OTTAWA FOOD

OTTAWA FOOD

A HUNGRY CAPITAL

DON CHOW & JENNIFER LIM

THE History PRESS

Published by The History Press
Charleston, SC 29403
www.historypress.net

All images courtesy of the authors unless otherwise noted.

First published 2014

Manufactured in the United States

ISBN 978.1.62619.458.8

Library of Congress CIP data applied for.

Notice: The information in this book is true and complete to the best of our knowledge. It is offered without guarantee on the part of the authors or The History Press. The authors and The History Press disclaim all liability in connection with the use of this book.

To our parents, who instilled in us a love for food, gardening, cooking and the importance of sitting down for a family meal each day.

CONTENTS

ACKNOWLEDGEMENTS

This book could not have been possible without the help and encouragement of so many people. First and foremost, we are grateful to Katie Orlando, our commissioning editor at The History Press, who took a chance on two unsuspecting kids who just happen to write about food in their spare time. All she knew of us when she offered us a book contract was what she saw on our blog, foodiePrints, and perhaps on social media. With every deadline we missed, her e-mails gave us the confidence that we could do it. We are humbled and still in shock that Katie approached us. Without her, this book wouldn't have happened. We are forever indebted to her.

Sincere thanks also go out to the many people who helped us along the way with our research, sharing their memories and time with us: Eugene Haslam, Pat Nicastro and Rocco Nicastro Jr., Kyrn Stein, Marysol Foucault, Dave Loan, Kyle Mortimer-Proulx, Danny Mongeon, Charles Beauregard, Tara Simpson, Linda Cook, Ian Reed, Giuliano Boselli, Craig Buckley, Paul Couvrette, Jantine Van Kregten, Andy Terauds, Jose Bento, Madan Sharma, George Monsour, Donna Bush, Patrick Garland, Paul Meek, Tracey Black, Stephen Beckta, Randy Fitzpatrick, Michael Blackie, Philip Powell, Jen Wall and Steve Wall, Kym Ng, Heather Hossie, Jason Duffy, Steph Legari, John Leung, Shane Clark, Rob McIssac, Richard Nigro, Patti Murphy, Sarah Burns and Phillippe Dupuy.

Restaurant critic Anne DesBrisay is someone we have looked up to over the years. Thank you for your encouragement and for lending us books and materials to help us with our research. You have been our inspiration for foodiePrints.

A big thank-you also goes to Jasmine for driving around town and picking up groceries as we buried ourselves in our writing. Jazzy, without you, we would have starved!

To our family and friends, having you cheer for us as we embarked on this adventure has been heartwarming. We love you dearly and are thankful to have you in our lives.

We would also like to give a special thank-you to librarian Brian Silcoff of the Ottawa Room at the Ottawa Public Library. You helped us smile when we were discouraged and frustrated with writers' block.

We are honoured to have been given this opportunity to write about our hometown. We hope that we have created something special. In the end, we offer this work to the efforts of those striving to make Ottawa into an extraordinary culinary destination.

INTRODUCTION

Over the years, Ottawa has gained a reputation as a mundane city due to its political nature. It did not help the city's image when a self-appointed committee of experts in Toronto for the Boring Awards named Ottawa the "Most Boring City" in Canada in 2013. Dull and forgettable, ours is a tedious existence, labouring in old office buildings filled with dusty cubicles and computer screens.

And food wise? With the city generally regarded as a culinary wasteland, people often joked that one had to leave town in order to get a decent meal. But those involved in the food and restaurant industry have worked hard over the years to shake off this unfortunate notoriety. They are working to develop Ottawa's culinary identity.

This book explores the local food scene from the 1980s until the present day. Once largely a landscape of pub grub, it slowly changed as Ottawans began dining out at classical French restaurants. Ethnic cuisine later emerged as immigration changed the face of Ottawa. We reacquainted ourselves with farming and eating and buying locally. Current food trends have forced us to rediscover our history of craft beer and explore street food with trucks and carts.

For far too long, Ottawa has been living under the shadows of Toronto and Montreal. It is time to celebrate and to take pride in our food. We are a city of farmers, artisan producers, chefs, microbrewers, restaurateurs and entrepreneurs. Determination and hard work are steadily turning Ottawa into something special—perhaps even a culinary destination.

This account strictly focuses on Ottawa, with some mentions of nearby Gatineau, Quebec and occasionally towns in the Ottawa Valley. Hull refers to present-day downtown Gatineau. Previously a city of its own standing, Hull merged with Gatineau to form the new city of Gatineau in 2002. Hull-Gatineau is generally considered a part of the National Capital Region. Many of the eateries and breweries featured still exist, although a number of businesses have closed or been replaced as the city transformed itself. While grocery stores, food businesses, farmers, breweries and restaurants are mentioned, there was simply not enough space to include them all.

Ottawa may not be a very old city, but it has such a rich history. It is our hope that the stories we've put together inspire you to try a new restaurant or cuisine, purchase more local foods, take a tour of a brewery, shop at a farmers' market or be more involved with your community.

Having lived in Ottawa all our lives, we were excited to get a chance to research and write about the past three decades. As we are scarcely older than the period in question, it has been fascinating learning how much Canada's capital has changed regarding food. Old memories surfaced, and aspects we took for granted—like dining in a completely smoke-free environment—were once contentious issues as city council strived to create a healthier city.

We are not professional writers, and we have never worked in the food or restaurant industries. But we are passionate about food and cooking. We read, breathe, dream and chat about food. We started off as food bloggers, writing about our cooking adventures and mishaps in the kitchen and sharing recipes with friends. From there, we began dining out and learned that Ottawa prepares and serves great food. We started meeting restaurateurs, chefs, cooks, servers, farmers and other local producers—all good people who work hard every day to create positive food experiences and lasting memories.

Regardless of where your interest lies, we hope that you find something tasty on every page.

Chapter 1

HUMBLE BEGINNINGS

Going back nearly forty years, Ottawa was a gastronomic wasteland. Suffering through dining out in Canada's capital during the decade leading to the 1980s arguably cemented Ottawa's reputation for being a food backwater. Recommending where to eat would involve urging people to cross the river into Hull. Better yet, keep driving until you arrive in Montreal.

Celebrated *Maclean's* columnist Allan Fotheringham deemed Ottawa the "City that Fun Forgot," "Coma City" and "Sparta on the Tundra" during his tenure covering federal politics in the early 1970s. He no doubt reviewed his notes from the latest media scrum outside the House of Commons while tucking into a platter of barbecued chicken, boiled vegetables, mashed potatoes and a dinner roll at Yesterday's on Sparks Street.

Perhaps it is a quirk of the English language that the Parliament of Canada and its administrative arm, the Government of Canada, get referred to as "Ottawa." When a city is associated with collecting income taxes, it earns a stereotype of being home to pencil pushers. Residents are perceived as either dutiful drones (broken by years of policy writing and briefing upwards) or self-important politicals (young, well coifed and aggressive, eagerly suckling at his or her elected master's teat). Proving the stereotype, mundane people ate mundane things. It would take two decades to instigate change.

What materialized during the 1980s and early 1990s—the locally owned and operated "chain"-style restaurants, the North American–adapted ethnic options and the continental-inspired finer dining—set a foundation for what would come next. Notably, the factors that changed how and what we ate then largely affect the culinary landscape now: the prevailing economy, immigration, municipal oversight and food trends from larger metropolitan centers. Above all, Ottawa demonstrated that it had an appetite for something more.

Explained Paul Couvrette, one of the city's more prominent photographers since Youssef Karsh, "Travelling home from London was disheartening. Looking out of the airplane window, I saw nothing!"[1]

Couvrette, whose family originally landed in what would become the National Capital Region in 1653, studied journalism at Carleton University. Graduating in 1973, he travelled throughout Europe and worked for Wallace Heaton at his eponymous camera shop in London, England (before it was purchased by Dixon's). Returning from his sojourn overseas, he was dubious about his hometown's dining options. "The ByWard Market was non-existent…there was nothing to eat," he continued.

A Tour of the ByWard Market

As the heart of Ottawa, the ByWard Market was a bit of an oasis from the 1970s-era office buildings that littered the downtown core, filled with dusty cubicles, padded swivel chairs, melamine desks and locked file cabinets. The "Market" would become a tourism and entertainment district.

According to Wim ten Hagen ten Holder, who owned Café Wim and Gallery on Sussex (chess sets, concerts, bikini shows and more) until its demise, there were three restaurants in "all the ByWard Market" in 1979: "Del Mar," Daphne and Victor's (47 William Street) and the Courtyard Restaurant (21 George Street).

Ten Holder's less-than-charitable generalization is somewhat untrue, as there was the Golden Dragon Tavern and Restaurant on Rideau Street (176), reputedly first to serve Chinese brunch "dim sum" staples. There was Café La Guillotine, a vast French restaurant situated down the street from where he would open Wim (513 Sussex). There was also Le Jardin (127 York), a lovingly converted brick house whose three "parlours" embodied exclusive fine dining; the Hayloft Steak and Seafood House (200 Rideau Street), a casual steakhouse that was established in 1972 with an in-house butcher; the Keg (75 York Street), a national chain steakhouse that took no reservations but offered a salad bar; the Old Spaghetti Factory (126 York Street), a national chain spaghetti house; and the Brandy's Room (just "Brandy's" to most), a "restaurant turned singles' bar by night" that was collocated with the Spaghetti Factory ("Order the 'shrimp and crabacado'!"). There were more than three restaurants, but, as Couvrette pointed out, there seemed limited variety.

Of those mentioned, only the venerable Courtyard Restaurant, a longstanding banquet hall that saw two fires, survives today. Originally a log tavern in 1827, the building was transformed into the McArther House Hotel. It went on to become McArther's British Hotel. Then, it was temporary lodging for the military during Confederation, the Clarendon House Hotel from 1875 to 1880 and headquarters for the Geological Survey of Canada. Ten Holder glimpsed repairs to the Courtyard after a fire in an adjoining building damaged restaurant renovations that had begun in 1978.

Deciding to introduce a less stuffy Dutch influence to Ottawa, he modelled Café Wim after Amsterdam's "brown" cafés. Years later, Peter Boole would see potential in its fifteen-foot ceilings and renovate the café, opening Social Restaurant in 1999. Boole's intention involved creating an upscale space where people could have dinner, drink at the bar or do both. Such sensibilities didn't exist in the 1980s.

While the ByWard Market was still a place to shop, eat and drink, the neighbourhood was more industrial, owing to the market being Ottawa's mercurial hub. Wholesalers and resellers joined struggling local farmers, retailing groceries to fellow businesses and Ottawa residents. Mostly generations-old family-run businesses, people sold goods to people.

Merchants around the ByWard Market Square, essentially one city block, sold meat, fish, cheese, deli-style products and produce. Daniel Bisson's family operated Albert's on William Street from 1956. His was a full-service butchery that supplied specialty items like racks of lamb and grain-fed chicken to the stately kitchens powering the residences of the governor general (Rideau Hall) and prime minister (24 Sussex).

There was J. Saso and Son's grocery store (64 George Street), Omer Hamway's House of Cheese (34 ByWard Market Square), Eric Vivian Jr.'s Lapointe Fish Market (46 ByWard Market Square), John Diener's Saslove's Meat Market (50 ByWard Market Square), Andre Vertes's Budapest Delicatessen (54 ByWard Market Square), Sam Zunder's Fruitland (60 ByWard Market Square) and Irving Swedko's the Fresh Fruit Company.

While Lapointe, the House of Cheese and Saslove's survive today in some form, J. Saso and Son's is now La Bottega Nicastro; Budapest Delicatessen is now a Wine Rack, a discount wine retailer; Zunder's Fruitland (originally

Zunder's Quality Fruit) is now an EQ3, an urban furniture store retailing loft-style furnishings and accents; and the Fresh Fruit Company is now Olive & Chili, a "grab and go" meal vendor.

In the evenings, outings in the ByWard Market tended to involve getting yourself a bite to eat on your way to the nearest bar or tavern. Back then, Ottawa's dining out scene was exemplified by the steakhouse. Italian food, particularly heavily sauced pasta entrées, was the mainstream ethnic option. Fine dining was represented by quasi-classical French options. Ottawa's food scene was also very much a local one, with obscure favourites distributed across the city.

Longtime local and restaurateur Charles Beauregard of Canvas Resto-Bar (65 Holland Avenue) in Hintonburg graduated from high school in 1986 before going on to Algonquin College for culinary school. He remembers the rise of the hot and cold buffets (Papa Joe's on Montreal Road); specialty crêpes (the Crêperie on York Street); all-you-could-eat salad bars; roast beef houses (Friday's on Elgin Street); imported Bindi desserts, served to diners on carts (Mamma Teresa on Somerset); and choose-your-own-adventure pasta plates, with a choice of eight different sauces (Fettuccine's, then on Bank Street).

Raised by a single parent, Beauregard dined out often with his mom, but inexpensively. A particular treat was visiting quirky I.P. Looney's in the east end, off St. Laurent Boulevard (1211 Joseph Cyr Street). A locally owned and operated family restaurant, its servers dressed up as cartoon or comic characters. "Management was known to cut off gentlemen's ties,"[2] described Beauregard. Patrons could be greeted by the Lone Ranger. Drink orders could be taken by Little Bo Peep. Zorro could serve. Superman would bus tables.

Looking back to its wordier ads, Looney's menu seemed a microcosm of Ottawa food: "I.P. Tizers" escargot, potato skins, nachos or chicken fingers; "garden fresh" vegetables in the salad bar; and prime rib, sirloin, "BBQ chicken," salmon, baked sole, veal parma "Looney" or "Brontosaurus" rib mains. Eventually, the cowboys would take over, and I.P. Looney's became a Lone Star Café.

Eugene Haslam, tireless independent music promoter and owner of Zaphod Beeblebrox (27 York Street), a live music venue and night club, arrived in Ottawa to work as a banker in 1977. A younger man then, he remembers frequenting Mamma Teresa (originally at 281 Kent Street) and former Peter's Pantry (1394 Richmond Road) and Saucy Noodle (409 Somerset Street West). Nearby to his Elgin Street office was Al's Steak House and the former Mayflower Restaurant and Pub. The Mayflower, where Haslam spent many a Friday evening with drink in hand, shut its doors in 2013 after thirty-five years in business.

"I built the Brigadier's Pump on York Street for Kanny Ng, who owned the Chinese Village Restaurant [and Tavern (415 Rideau Street)]. [The Pump] was an English pub, but we wanted to offer a Canadian experience."[3] Located at 23 York Street, the Brigadier's Pump originally served steak and kidney pie and curried chicken. A bit of a speakeasy, its entrance was obscured. The Pump is now the Brig Pub and is renowned for its wings and beer.

The Darling

The "darling restaurant" of the 1980s was Daphne and Victor's. In 1978, Daphne Birks and Victor Chan opened a counterculture café with "European"-inspired décor at 47 William Street. Its brick-exposed walls were adorned with Oriental rugs and antique mirrors. The cozy dining room consisted of padded deuces and four-tops. Besides some twists on the standard continental menu of the time, Daphne and Victor's served burgers, but these were not your ordinary griddled quarter-pounders with cheese on sesame seed buns. Humble patties were adorned with creamy béchamel or sautéed mushrooms and finished in Burgundy (the "Romanoff"). Think lamb burgers with goat cheese and vegetarian pecan burgers with a cheddar Mornay sauce. Accepting no reservations but value priced, the café drew legions of the under-thirty crowd, resulting in unheard-of lineups at lunch and dinner.

Explained Richard Nigro, Domus Café's original day chef and later cofounder of Juniper Kitchen and Wine Bar, "There was very little in Ottawa in the early 1980s: classic French [restaurants]; steakhouses; some Canadian Chinese food; and Daphne and Victor's. They served gourmet hamburgers and 'real' fries."[4] The café was also known for its European coffee, market soups (a favourite of students) and pastries. Apparently, its Sunday brunch menu sported a very respectable eggs Florentine.

Peggy Bradley took over Daphne and Victor's in 1987, opening the multistory William Street Café. Recipes for her café's salads and soups are still sought after today, like its curried carrot soup with white wine and Greek salad with black olives, Boston lettuce and minced onion-spiked balsamic dressing. The pecan burger recipe that she inherited remained a trade secret for years, although Bradley used more expensive skinless almonds in the nut burgers she served.

Carmen Letourneau opened former Café Paradiso in 1999. A trendy café in downtown Ottawa (199 Bank Street), Paradiso served California-style cuisine. Part café and part lounge, it hosted many a jazz band in the evening. Its menu featured classy comfort staples like burgers, personal pizzas, panini, pastas and salads. Its house salad consisted of arugula, pears, prosciutto chips, grilled leeks, Asiago cheese and an orange-ginger dressing. One of Paradiso's pizzas featured grilled spiced chicken, an onion marmalade and a yogurt dressing. A conspicuous addition to the menu was "Peggy's Pecan Burger." More surprising, Letourneau released the guarded recipe to the *Ottawa Citizen*'s Jane Stratton in a vegetarian burger roundup that was published in September 2000.

THE RITZ ANOMALY

By 1986, the corporation that owned and operated the Old Spaghetti Factory and Brandy's had declared the two businesses bankrupt. The once popular restaurant and bar had been acquired by then struggling The Keg restaurant chain, which was in the process of reorganizing to regain profitability.

The Keg was the major shareholder and principal creditor, owed $425,000. The businesses owed another $375,000 to others. Their closure put seventy employees out of work. Then Keg president Brad Bond told the *Ottawa Citizen*'s Janice Middleton that there were a number of restaurants for sale in Ottawa and little interest. For Brandy's, it simply fell out of favour with the ByWard Market. Drinkers opted for competing roadhouse-style taverns instead. For the Spaghetti Factory, diners' appetites changed. The baby boomers who crowded the restaurant in the late 1970s and early 1980s were adopting healthier lifestyles that didn't include large plates of cheap pasta.

Explained restaurateur George Monsour, "The Spaghetti Factory was about entertainment; not nourishment. Cheap drinks; not gastronomy."[5] He added, pausing and smiling, "Actually, I met Donna working there." Both servers, Monsour and Donna Bush keenly observed how everything operated at the Old Spaghetti Factory, learning how to (and how not to) run a restaurant. The lessons they gleaned would come in handy.

Monsour grew up in the industry. His father worked as a short-order cook and his mother as a dishwasher when they arrived in Ottawa from Lebanon in 1957. Young George remembers living above a number of the restaurants that his father successively opened. One was Mirella on Laurier Avenue where the Esplanade Laurier office towers now stand. "Ottawa was a sleepy town back then. At Mirella, we served hot sandwiches with gravy, grilled cheese with pickles, club sandwiches, coffee and muffins."

Before the Old Spaghetti Factory, Monsour worked as a dishwasher and overnight prep cook. Then he worked as a bartender at the Hayloft. Sporting a butcher's coat and a straw hat, he served Harvey Wallbanger cocktails, the hip thing to drink, to anyone saddling up to the in-house bar, called "Le Shed." Originally a convent, whose chapel now resides in the National Gallery of Canada, the concrete building that became the Hayloft was eventually redeveloped into condos after it closed. The steakhouse would change hands in 1988 and closed in 1993.

Bush was new to the industry. Born in Montreal, she worked at the Old Spaghetti Factory to pay for her psychology studies at Carleton University.

The future couple would lose touch with each other for a number of years, with Bush moving to Toronto. He remained, moving on to the Atlantic Pavilion seafood restaurant on Slater Street (253), becoming assistant floor manager. When they met again, Monsour and Bush would launch a small empire in November 1981, taking over a failed venture by Daphne Birks and Victor Chan on Elgin Street (274) called the Ritz. He borrowed $7,000 from his parents. She contributed $3,000. They bought the restaurant, mortgaging the value of the kitchen equipment and recycling the branding.

What became Ritz 3, "third" after the luxury hotel and the Nabisco cracker, was revolutionary at the time because its Italian-inspired fare was entirely made from scratch, including the desserts. Monsour hired Raffaela (Bella) Milito for the kitchen. Together, they used the four and a half months between the restaurant's opening and its becoming licensed to serve alcohol to learn how to roll and cut fresh pasta efficiently. She would go on to open Bella's Bistro Italiano in a converted two-story house on Wellington Street West (1445) in 1995.

Elsewhere downtown, Cindy Toffanello Yabar had just opened a pasta shop with an L-shaped restaurant area that sat thirty people behind it on Bank Street (199). Yabar and her then fiancé Luchio gambled with their wedding funds, purchasing and renovating what was originally a sandwich shop called Hockey Submarine. Fettuccine's would attract many customers, who lined up for takeout and to dine-in, necessitating expanding into nearby retail space. Wholesale demands from other businesses would force them to establish a factory on Star Top Road.

The Ritz menu would list dishes like "Pane con Pesto" (house-made bread, topped with pesto, tomatoes and mozzarella), "Insalata di Carciofi e Funghi" (mushroom and artichoke heart salad), "Scaloppine Bentivoglio" (veal in mushroom cream sauce with garlic and parsley) and "Cannelloni con Ricotta e Spinaci" (spinach- and ricotta-filled cannelloni).

Kathleen Walker of the *Ottawa Citizen* newspaper, Ottawa's former restaurant reviewer, described it as "revitalized Italian cuisine." She would actually pursue Monsour for the recipe for his "Zuccotto Cake" for years.

At its peak in 1987, Monsour and Bush operated five wildly successful Ritz restaurants across Ottawa: the original on Elgin Street, a second Ritz 3 on Bank Street (1665), the Ritz Pizzeria on Clarence Street, Tidbitz on Nepean Street (226) and the Canal Ritz on Queen Elizabeth Driveway.

The Ritz 3 (thirty-two seats) on Bank Street was originally Nick's, a restaurant that Monsour opened for his parents before they retired. The salad girl he hired for the location, Tracey Clark, would go on to help him manage the day-to-day operations of his growing empire, streamlining and developing programs of processes and procedures. Years later, Clark would use some of these skills to manage iconic Bridgehead Coffee.

The Ritz Pizzeria on Clarence Street was more of a "success breeds necessity" expansion. The central bakery beneath the original Ritz was unable to keep up with the growing bread requirements of the satellite restaurants. Former dishwasher turned pastry chef Peter Langlois became a partner, baker and part-time pizzaiolo. Monsour had a wood-burning oven put in, thinking it a first. In a twist of fate, Vincenzo Piazza of the Ottawa Bagel Shop had his installed several weeks before, so the Ritz could only ever boast of operating the first wood-burning "pizza" oven in Ontario.

Tibitz (sixty seats) on Nepean Street was formerly the failed La Maison. There, Monsour hired Yannick Vincent, former chef of 24 Sussex (Pierre Trudeau and Joe Clark era), to consult. Tibitz became a wine bar, serving French-inspired small plates like "Escargots au Roquefort." A young Stephen Beckta would open his flagship restaurant in the location in 2003.

The Canal Ritz (seventy-five seats) was an expensive crown jewel. Against his better judgment, Monsour installed a kitchen and ordered the necessary renovations to open a restaurant in the building. The wood-fired pizza oven that he hastily installed had to be rebuilt thereafter. This location had no parking.

By its fifth year, the Ritz chain saw annual revenues of $5 million and employed two hundred people. Monsour, a self-described "philosopher restaurateur," went on to implement a no-smoking policy at the Ritz restaurants he solely owned a decade before the City of Ottawa instituted its groundbreaking bylaw. He even experimented with opening a take-home food shop in the bedroom community of Orleans at the Town Centre (240 Centrum Boulevard) and making house wines (Riesling and Chardonnay) for his restaurants.

Eventually, exhausted from dealing with municipal and provincial red tape and frustrated with restaurant operations, he and Bush slowly divested their ownership of the Ritz restaurants. In 1990, Kalil Saikely of Hull-based Sirolas Steak House bought the Canal Ritz. In 1995, Jimmy Saikely, who bought the Tibitz on Nepean and turned it into a Ritz 3, took over the original on Elgin.

Monsour and Bush, newly married, moved to France to raise their children. Dabbling in modern point-of-sale systems and supply chain automation while putting on the Ritz, he opened a software firm. Monsour would return to Ottawa in 2011, opening Back Lane Café in the trendy Hintonburg neighbourhood on Wellington Street West.

Grocery Wars

"I couldn't buy cilantro at the Loblaws!" exclaimed Eugene Haslam. "There was no oyster sauce or curry pastes [at the grocery stores]."

Indeed, at the time, the major Ottawa-area supermarkets were more interested fighting one another in price wars over milk, eggs, sugar and butter for the loyalty of shoppers. Large chain grocery stores were still establishing themselves in the city, strategically installing locations in suburban neighbourhoods. In 1986, four stores—Loblaws, IGA, A&P and Dominion—were selling four-litre bags of 2 percent milk for $2.29 and a dozen large eggs for $1.29. The price war that would affect all food retail began that January when IGA promised to freeze prices on eighty-six items until April 2. Steinberg and Mr. Grocer would enter the fray.

Moses Loeb, a young Russian immigrant who paid $200 for a small store at Ottawa's LeBreton Flats in 1912, launched the grocery empire that brought the first Independent Grocers Alliance (IGA) stores to Ottawa. At its helm then was Bertram Loeb, Moses's son. As president and then CEO, Bertram bought the first IGA regional franchise to Canada.

Eventually, new shareholders would take over the company in 1977, forcing him to resign as chairman. Quebec supermarket chain Provigo later took control, dropping the IGA name and, adding insult to injury, rebranding all stores to "Loeb."

Forty-one Ottawa Loeb stores would be bought by Metro Inc. from Loblaws, which had acquired ailing Provigo in 1999. Loeb stores disappeared when Metro went on to rename all stores under its portfolio in 2008, including Dominon and A&P. At its height, M. (Moses) Loeb Ltd. directly employed 1,800 employees.

Still, for cilantro, oyster sauce or curry pastes, Eugene Haslam had to visit an independent ethnic store. It wasn't until 1994 that marketing experts advised grocery chains to start catering to ethnic shoppers.

ITALIAN GROCERY CONNECTION

In Ottawa, there are several longstanding food retail institutions known to Italian immigrants and their children: Pasticceria Gelateria Italiano (200 Preston Street), Luciano's Fine Foods (114 Preston Street) and "Nicastro's." For pasta, you will be pointed to Home of Fresh Pasta (106 Preston Street) or Parma Ravioli (1314 Wellington Street West).

Suffice it to say, the name "Nicastro" is synonymous with Italian foodstuffs. There is Nicastro's Italian Food Emporium (Nicastro Fine Foods) at 1558 Merivale Road, La Bottega Nicastro at 64 George Street and Il Negozio Nicastro at either 1355 Wellington Street West or 792 Bank Street.

While members have drifted apart over the years, Nicastro's is a family business originally founded by six brothers. Together, the now extended family can boast five generations of experience in food retail.

Everything began when Frank Nicastro Sr. left his village of Cleto in southern Italy for Canada in 1962. He landed in Ottawa and worked in construction as a carpenter for the next four years. One by one, his five siblings followed his example: Giuseppe (Joe), Ugo, Allesandro (Alexander), Salvatore (Sam) and Rocco Sr.

When Frank Sr. had saved enough seed money to start a business, he opened tiny Frank's Meat and Grocery on Somerset Street West. The original intention was to return to Italy and open a store, something akin to their father's Alimentari, which the patriarch operated until his passing in 1967.

According to Willy Barth of the *Ottawa Citizen*, each brother took on a role at Frank's. Allesandro, who had been a butcher in the old country, took over ordering meat. Salvatore bought produce. Ugo was the "receiver." Rocco did the bookkeeping and purchasing. Frank ran the operation. Joe traveled to Ottawa in 1966. Only sixteen years old, he started off in construction as well, but he helped out at Frank's. Joe looked after the delicatessen.

When the brothers managed to save $50,000, they looked into a joint venture in 1971. One year later, the brothers expanded into a Gladstone Avenue store, filling the 3,200-square-foot building with meat, fresh produce and specialty Italian products. Nicastro's Brothers Foods was opened to service Italian families in a growing Little Italy.

Joe's son, Pasquale (Pat), explained that the Gladstone store became a mainstay for Italian grocery despite smaller shops opening along Preston Street. The brothers paid off the building's mortgage in ten years. Pat joined the family business at the tender age of twelve years old, helping out however he could. "I grew up selling olives [at Nicastro's Brothers Foods],"[6] he reminisced wistfully.

Although they sold their Somerset operation in 1977, the family continues to own the building at 564 Gladstone. The current tenants are also in the food retail business: Jo-Ann Laverty and Jennifer Heagle of fine food shop Red Apron. However, Laverty and Heagle's business model has more to do with operating a café and retailing locavore take-home dinner solutions.

When Ottawa's Italian families began establishing themselves during the latter half of the 1970s, finding meaningful employment and having children, they moved westward into the former municipality of Nepean, creating a new ethnic hub. So, the brothers expanded again into retail space on Merivale Road.

For a time, both Gladstone and Merivale stores operated simultaneously, retailing 150 different cheeses (including Pecorella, Friulano, Parmigiano and Gorgonzola); sixteen varieties of house-marinated olives from Spain, Italy, Greece and Algeria; and twelve varietals of grapes for winemaking.

Finally, some of the brothers branched out into a six-thousand-square-foot space one block from the original on Merivale, opening Nicastro Fine

Foods. Part deli, part specialty food shop, part coffee bar and part catering, this location persists today. The family owns the plaza.

Unwilling to compete with big-box grocery (Steinberg's at the time), neither Merivale location stocked traditional grocery items. Nicastro Fine Foods stocks Italian favourites like Genova salami, prosciutto di Parma and amaretto cookies. It offers customized gift baskets with artisan products. It continues to offer one of Ottawa's largest selections of imported cheeses.

Pat's father explained to Iris Winston of the *Ottawa Citizen* in 2000 that his was a personal touch. "We treat customers like family and friends," Pat continued. "We form relationships."

Joe and his brothers were always resident owners, on hand seven days a week to welcome customers. Almost 75 percent being regulars, they knew their shoppers by name. The brothers' hard work sent the first generation of Canadian-born Nicastro children to university.

Salvatore's son Robert studied at Carleton University and graduated with a political science degree. In 1994, Robert was in the midst of a career as political staff for a federal Member of Parliament. On the side, he opened Pesto's Deli & Fresh Pasta in the west end suburb of Kanata (471 Hazeldean Road). Now in its twentieth year, Pesto's retails deli products and takeout meals with fresh pasta and sauce.

In 1999, Robert left politics and, with brother David, opened Il Negozio Nicastro ("Nicastro's Store") in the Glebe neighbourhood (792 Bank Street). Theirs was a long and skinny shop with an old-fashioned look and feel. Unlike Nicastro Fine Foods, the Bank Street Il Negozio sells fresh produce. Brother Michael joined in 2004 to help expand Il Negozio into the West Wellington Village neighbourhood. Salvatore owns the building at 1355 Wellington Street West.

While Pesto's has a twenty-five-seat café, Il Negozio on Wellington opened with a full-service restaurant. Caffe Ventuno, named after Halifax's Pier 21, where Salvatore landed when he came to Canada, was originally staffed by Chef Michael Cummings of former Trattoria Zingaro. The restaurant served thin-crust pizzas, fresh pastas (like seared scallops on linguine or pasta puttanesca with monkfish) and battered and fried smelts with pepperoncini, garnering positive reviews from local restaurant critics. However, that location was renovated in 2013, closing down Caffe Ventuno. The Wellington Street Il Negozio still retains its two-hundred-cheese "boutique" but now includes an espresso bar and increased "grab and go" meal options. Also featured is Michael's house-made porchetta, which he retails under the "Bootleg Porchetta Company" brand.

Pat also studied at Carleton and graduated in 1995 from its business school. His fourth-year project involved opening La Bottega Nicastro in the ByWard Market. In fact, he wrote his last exams as renovations were being made to what was formerly J. Saso and Son's grocery store. Joseph's son, Charlie Saso, asked the Nicastros to continue his family's longstanding tradition of retailing Italian groceries downtown. The store was established in 1923 and began as a wholesale fruit operation. It was one of the ByWard Market's oldest stores.

La Bottega was an immediate success, stocking deli, imported cheeses and Italian staples. Pat insisted on installing a café and selling sandwiches. The sandwiches are made from the same meats and cheeses sold at the deli counter. "We always have a group of 'nonnas' working the café," said Pat. "[S]omebody's nonna, not necessarily ours. We serve well-priced home-style Italian food—food we ate at home. The store is their pantry. The sandwiches, they just took off! We couldn't make them fast enough."

In a bit of history repeating itself, Pat's cousin Rocco Jr. started working at La Bottega at age twelve, putting fliers on parked cars every Saturday. He is now a partner.

In 2007, Pat expanded La Bottega into the souvenir shop next door. He installed a sandwich counter and espresso bar. Suffice it to say, the store is still packed with locals from Ottawa's downtown core. Like their fathers, Pat and Rocco Jr. cultivated a clientele of regulars. Police officers stop in. So do firefighters, politicians, restaurateurs, chefs and the odd celebrity. Some have been visiting the convivial atmosphere of La Bottega for fifteen years. They bring their children.

Regarding La Bottega's success, Pat attributes everything to sourcing quality products and delivering value. "Back in the day, Italian immigrants bought in bulk. Mom cooked at home." While more important in his father's store, both the Nicastro Fine Foods and La Bottega retail Nicastro-branded olive oil, tomato sauces, pastas, vinegar and coffee. As staples imported from Italy, they are value priced. "We track the price point of products at every [big-box] chain store to stay competitive. Here [at La Bottega], we offer premium products, like more expensive Tuscan olive oil and aged balsamic vinegar."

Accordingly, La Bottega's ability to weather difficult economic conditions has to do with listening to customers and retailing a spectrum of products. "We have everything from $200/kg ibérico ham to $6 sandwiches. Everyone travels. We provide reminders of what they had in Italy." He continued, "When restaurants feel 'the pinch,' we sell more groceries, so people can have special meals at home. When the economy [is good], people buy higher-end groceries."

The Nicastros also adapted to accommodate their clientele. While Joe started offering more prepared foods for the busy dual-income family, Pat offers products for the more discerning palate. Rocco is fluently trilingual (English, Italian and French), so he can speak with his customers.

When La Bottega opened, there were "For Sale" and "For Lease" signs in abundance in the ByWard Market. Market vendors had been decimated in the early 1990s thanks to the municipal government's "market value assessment" initiative, equalizing property taxes to 1988 levels. Recession battered, vendors were already fighting a price war with one another, on-street resellers and chain grocery stores. Higher property values, sometimes 175 percent higher, meant higher property taxes. Higher property taxes forced many out of business.

Pat gambled on the ByWard Market bouncing back. Young professionals have since moved into nearby condo developments. Empty-nesters are returning from the suburbs. He and Rocco Jr. are now gambling on the high-rise condo buildings being erected off Preston Street. Returning to Little Italy, they plan to expand La Bottega into a second location under Domecile's Nuovo Building. It should open in 2016.

RISE OF CHINESE AND VIETNAMESE FOOD

For a city hosting so many embassies and diplomats, the makeup of Ottawa's early food scene lacked an underlying ethnic food baseline. Being Canada's capital, it should be representatively multicultural.

Mostly, Canadian Chinese restaurants were prevalent: Cathay Restaurant (228 Albert Street), Golden Palace (2195 Carling Avenue), former Lucky Key (1272 Carling Avenue), Ho Ho Restaurant (875 Richmond Road) and Ruby Inn (1834 Bank Street).

Former Cathay, with its gold façade and silhouetted emerald green dragon, seemed out of place on Albert Street in the downtown core. In fact, a four-block stretch of Albert, intersecting at thoroughfare Bank Street, was Chinatown in the 1950s. Then, the half dozen Chinese-owned and operated businesses included confectioneries, small grocery stores and other restaurants. Cathay and its chop suey house brethren have a legacy. They

The old signage belonging to Cathay Restaurant is still visible along Albert Street in downtown Ottawa.

were the natural evolution of the cafés opened by sojourning Chinese who came to Canada to work before 1962.

On July 1, 1923, the Government of Canada repealed the Head Tax, enacting the Chinese Immigration Act (also known as the Exclusion Act). While the Head Tax made emigrating from China prohibitively expensive, the Exclusion Act made it illegal. The legislation also denied all resident Chinese, immigrant or Canadian-born, the right to be naturalized. When Prime Minister William Lyon Mackenzie King repealed the act twenty-four years later, he defended maintaining restrictions to prevent changing the country's demographic makeup.

Faced with painful isolation and institutionalized discrimination, one of the few businesses landed Chinese could open were cafés. At first, the tiny establishments served North American fare like hot sandwiches and freshly cut fries. Then, resourceful families adapted mostly southern Chinese dishes for western palates, employing available ingredients.

Soups and sauces were thicker than Cantonese recipes considered authentic by Chinese immigrants. Vegetables were quickly blanched and stir-fried. Proteins were battered and deep-fried. Flavours were blander but sweeter. A new cuisine was born.

Many cafés became full-service restaurants and prospered, serving General Tso's chicken, wonton soup, hot and sour soup, sweet and sour pork, chicken balls, ginger beef, beef and broccoli, crispy beef, egg rolls and lemon chicken. Takeout restaurants opened. Suffice it to say, when early restaurant reviews described food as "real Chinese cooking," it usually meant that the Chinese cooks in the kitchen were "real," rather than imaginary. The food was accordingly not.

Beginning in the late 1970s, this would change. Ottawa experienced an influx of immigration into what would become the Somerset Heights neighbourhood, especially via former mayor Marion Dewer's Project 4000 relief effort to resettle Southeast Asian "boat people" who were displaced by war. She is now celebrated for her role in organizing the local community to sponsor four thousand refugees from Vietnam, Cambodia and Laos. In the 1990s, Hong Kong immigrants would follow due to the former British colony reverting to China in 1997.

The small cluster of Chinese businesses expanded, causing some resentment from surrounding homeowners. City developers cited gentrification as a reason why entrepreneurs should not be granted the required permits to build new "Chinese" restaurants in the area. Restaurants would displace retail businesses or housing.

Eventually, the six-block neighbourhood grew to host numerous Asian restaurants (Chinese, Vietnamese, Korean, Japanese and Thai), groceries, gift shops and other small businesses. One of the longstanding restaurants, Mekong (637 Somerset Street West), was opened by former Project 4000 refugee Dennis Luc in 1985.

Luc arrived in Ottawa at age fifteen and got his start in the restaurant industry, working at Yang Sheng Restaurant (662 Somerset Street West), cleaning ducks for a quarter each. Originally, he intended two-story Mekong to be a pho noodle house, one of three on Chinatown's main drag. Unfortunately, 1980s diners had little interest in Vietnamese food, so he slowly dumped the menu in favour of North American Chinese fare. Only rice paper rolls and deep-fried spring rolls remain. Joined by his wife, Ruby Cheng, in 1991, they added more dishes, including Peking duck. Luc worked the back of house. Cheng coordinated the menu and worked the front of house, with its linen tables and elaborate table settings.

Service is why Cheng feels Mekong has outlasted so many of the restaurants in the neighbourhood. But with a proliferating Vietnamese community, pho noodle houses would begin to appear by the dozen elsewhere on Somerset Street in coming years.

A monument sits in a garden in Chinatown. It is dedicated to the four thousand refugees who settled in Ottawa.

Mekong is one of the longstanding restaurants in Chinatown.

Ruby Cheng brings a taste of Mekong for a pop-up dinner event at Mellos Diner.

Deeply flavourful pho soup is made from slowly simmering bones and meat, onions, ginger and some characteristic spices: cloves, star anise, cinnamon and coriander seeds. Usually beef-based (pho bo) or chicken-based (pho ga), the soup can also be flavoured with black peppercorns, black cardamom and fennel seeds. It is sweetened with rock sugar and finished with fish sauce. A departure from authentic-to-local bowls in Vietnam, patrons can opt for enormous portions with a large variety of "toppings," like braised brisket, fatty sliced beef, beef balls, sliced beef tendon, sliced chicken or boiled quail eggs. With the bowls of soup noodle inexpensive to make, a number of entrepreneurs succeeded where Luc failed.

Presently, there are Vietnamese noodle houses in neighbourhoods across Ottawa, like Kanata Noodle House (500 Hazeldean Road) and Ox Head Restaurant (790 Kanata Avenue) in the west end. Many also serve Vietnamese comfort staples like spicy lemon grass/braised beef brisket stew (bo kho), spicy bun bo hue noodle soups and hu tieu noodle soups.

Before the pho houses took over, Gilbert Tam opened a three-hundred-seat banquet hall restaurant called Fuliwah in a newly renovated two-story brick building with a green tiled roof in 1986. Complete with a sweeping stairway and crystal chandeliers, ostentatious Fuliwah (704 Somerset Street

West) served Chinese food more recognizable to Hong Kong expats. This was one of two restaurants in which the Asian community celebrated special occasions. Similar Italian banquet halls (La Roma and Allegro) had been established in the neighbourhood for decades. Not wanting to alienate anyone, Tam had two enormous menus. More familiar North American Chinese food was available too.

Unfortunately, the business declared bankruptcy twelve years later, owing approximately $850,000 to creditors. A combination of high rent and low turnover during the 1990–91 recession felled the ornate restaurant. Sik Kwok Chu of rival Chu Sing restaurant across the street would expand into the space, investing hundreds of thousands of dollars into renovations. One of the renovations installed an elevator to help aging Chinatown residents get up to the dining room.

Across the street, Kym Ng, a third-generation restaurateur looks on from the family-run Yangtze Dining Lounge (700 Somerset Street West). She and her family watched Chinatown grow and develop. Yangtze, Ottawa's first Chinese banquet hall restaurant, was opened in 1982 by Ng's late grandfather, Choo Leung. "La Roma Restaurant used to be across the street in the '80s,"[7] she said, pointing to what is now a Pizza Pizza location at the corner of Bronson and Somerset (673 Somerset Street West).

Ng grew up working in her grandfather's first restaurant, a large North American Chinese buffet house called Dragon on Montreal Road. The family would divest the property in the 2000s after operating it successfully for thirty years. Interestingly, she and her father, Ricky, would go on to open Bambu Restaurant (3993 Riverside Drive) in the strip mall with new-to-Ottawa T&T Supermarket in the south end. Bambu serves upscale takes on westernized Thai, Chinese and Japanese fare, from maki-rolls to Thai curry chicken and stuffed eggplant.

Now, Ng manages the front of house at Yangtze. Her sixty-one-year-old father still works shifts in its busy eight- to ten-person kitchen. During brunch rushes, two cooks are dedicated to just making shrimp har gow and pork siu mai dumplings.

"When we took over this place, it was an Italian restaurant [too]. There were no windows. The interior was painted red; it was dark inside," Ng noted. "[Back then] we were very busy Fridays and Saturdays with lineups out the door until 2:00 a.m. But we really didn't compete with Fuliwah across the street. There was more than enough business. Everyone was happy."

Ricky would renovate Yangtze again in 1989, extending the dining room to the back of the building that the family now owns. Renovations

The Chinatown Royal Arch was built as a partnership between the Chinatown BIA, donors, three levels of government, the Chinese embassy and the City of Beijing.

also included painting the interior green and installing the familiar dragon and phoenix.

While Yangtze is no longer as busy as it once was, it has opted to do takeout, delivery, banquets, weddings and catering. "We are the official Chinese caterers to the Lac Leamy Hilton next to the Casino," Ng explained. She credits the longevity of Yangtze to quality ingredients and service that customers have become accustomed to for decades. "Everything is made from scratch! During the week between Christmas and New Year, we can go through 800 to 1,200 pounds of shrimp."

For the many people who grew up in Ottawa, dining at Yangtze has become a tradition. Some newly retired regulars bus in from the suburbs every day. Ng gestures discreetly at an elderly couple who spend up to two hours bussing each way just to have dim sum every week. Ottawa expats return to dine when they visit the city. Children who dined with their parents at Yangtze in the 1980s and early 1990s now bring their children. On any given day, it is not unusual to see a family of three generations at a table.

Already fluent in two other Chinese dialects, along with English and French, Ng mentions that she has had to pick up Mandarin. More Mandarin-speaking Chinese now make Ottawa their home. Also, tourists from China increased significantly following the granting of "Approved Destination Status" to Canada in June 2010.

However, like any long-running restaurant, its loyal customers are getting older. To attract new customers and establish the relationships that will make them regulars, the menu now includes vegetarian and gluten-free options. A handful of frequently requested Thai fusion dishes have also been added to the menu.

RISE OF THAI FOOD

Some credit Chef Art Akarapanich with bringing Thai food to Ottawa in 1980 when he opened Siam Kitchen on Bank Street (1050) near Old Ottawa South. Nine years later, he opened Siam Bistro on Wellington Street West in the West Wellington Village.

Locals embraced Chef Akarapanich's food, with diners often needing to make reservations, particularly at the Wellington Street location. Former food reviewer Kathleen Walker described the fare at the Siam restaurants as "colourful and so distinctively flavoured."

Accordingly, Akarapanich, a Thai national who would go on to open and operate three restaurants in Bangkok in the early 1990s, wanted to showcase the complexities of Thai cuisine, balancing sweet and sour and spicy and salty flavours.

At Siam, he employed Thai chiles, fresh cilantro, lemon grass, galangal, shallots, zest of kaffir limes, sweet basil and coconut milk. Diners were served plates with a fork and spoon, traditional utensils. Akarapanich would sell the Siam restaurants to Alice and Philip Lai, former proprietors of Ta Tung at 1353 Cyrville Road, before returning to Thailand with his pregnant wife. When he returned, he bought Marco Polo Restaurant on Bank Street (1585 Bank Street), renovating it to open Sweet Basil in 1996.

In 2001, hearing that the government of Thailand had ambitious plans to franchise five thousand "authentic" Thai restaurants around the world, Akarapanich and a number of other local restaurateurs would admit to westernizing Thai flavours. Having discovered that "North American palates," especially those of Ottawa's diners, weren't yet accustomed to the strong flavours or heat at Sweet Basil, Akarapanich set up the menus at his forthcoming ventures differently. Thai fare at Anna Fine Thai on Holland Avenue (91) and the Green Papaya Restaurants toned down the pungency and spice.

Participating in the proliferation of Thai restaurants in Ottawa during the 2000s, Akarapanich would go on to open Bangkok Noodle House (125 Bank Street), Sacred Garden (1300 Bank Street) and Som Tum (260 Nepean Street).

FALL OF FRENCH CUISINE

To celebrate special occasions, there were few fine dining options in Ottawa before former Egyptian-born nuclear physicist Adel Ayad began dabbling in the food service business in 1978. The newspapers of the time seem to like describing him as eccentric, extremely hard working and full of joie de vivre. His lauded Clair de Lune restaurant would close in 2005 after twenty-four years, having served celebrities like Marlen Cowpland (wife to Michael Cowpland, founder of Ottawa-based Canadian software company Corel) and Sir Peter Ustinov and dignitaries like Pierre Trudeau and Jean Chrétien.

According to his farewell interview in the *Ottawa Citizen*, Cowpland adored Claire de Lune's mashed potatoes. According to Ayad's relinquished recipe, the potatoes were mashed, passed through a drum sieve and then enriched with a cup of 35 percent cream. Indulgent, it is no wonder they became a favourite.

However, Claire de Lune was not Ayad's first venture. The legendary restaurateur opened Ottawa's first outdoor café, Marche du Soleil Café, one summer. Former food reviewer Kathleen Walker remembered that he served dishes like braised sweetbreads with capers in vol-au-vent shells. Three years later, after he quit his day job, Ayad would tempt diners, serving rabbit legs stuffed with duck liver mousseline in two sauces and risotto from Clarence Street.

It was 1981. Interest rates were 20 percent. Opening a full-service restaurant during a recession (1981–82), especially a higher-end one, was unheard of. After Margaret Trudeau, then wife of Liberal prime minister Trudeau, visited, however, cabinet ministers followed. Claire de Lune would earn mention in *Chatelaine* magazine. That's when the lineups for dinner started.

Three years later, Ayad expanded his restaurant, doubling his seating to forty-eight and adding a rooftop terrace. The terrace would become a signature feature for the former Firestone Restaurant Group's Stella Osteria, which took over the space after Clair de Lune shut down.

During its tenure, Claire de Lune's kitchen served classical French cuisine, "nouvelle" cuisine and "Market" cuisine (post-nouvelle cuisine, employing local ingredients). Ayad's menu changed seasonally.

Jason Duffy, who was born in Ottawa and raised in Gatineau, remembers returning to the National Capital Region during the late 1990s after completing his culinary training at Montreal's Institut de Tourisme et d'Hôtellerie du Québec. Having just completed his stage in France, he applied to work at Claire de Lune. "The stations and the technique, it was all classical French,"[8] he explained. Duffy is presently the executive chef at the ARC Lounge at ARC The Hotel (140 Slater).

French technique, which continues to be taught at culinary schools, serves as the foundation for finer cuisine today. Classical French cuisine, however, was alive and well in 1985, when Ottawa could finally compete on par with Hull for diners.

On the Hull side, Robert Bourassa bought, renovated and reopened Café Henry Burger during the summer of 1982, vowing to restore the Hull restaurant's reputation. The restaurant had been under varied ownership after the passing of Madame Marie Burger in 1973. The original café was opened by Madame's late husband back in 1922. Known for its fine French fare, it would move to rue Laval in 1929; fire relocated it to rue Laurier (69) in 1942. During Bourassa's tenure, Café Henry Burger experienced a rebirth, both in popularity and accolades, again drawing celebrities, prime ministers and the region's statesmen. One of Bourassa's former protégés, talented George Laurier, would go on to open competing Laurier Sur Montcalm (199 rue Montcalm). Some, including Ottawa restaurant critic Anne DesBrisay, formerly of the *Ottawa Citizen* newspaper, still believe that Laurier's grasp of French cuisine surpassed that of his former chef.

The same year renovations were being made to Bourassa's café, Jean-Pierre Mueller became disenchanted with working for the American embassy. Until then, he had served as chef for seven consecutive ambassadors over seventeen years. When Paul Robinson took the post, Mueller discovered that Mrs. Robinson preferred hamburgers and French fries to steak tartare and pommes dauphinoise. So, he took his leave and opened Chez Jean-Pierre with his wife, Rachel, at 210 Somerset Street West on October 5, 1982.

Well regarded for his devotion to classic and not "nouvelle," Chez Jean-Pierre became celebrated amongst food critics and the fine dining crowd, garnering successive positive reviews. Most mention excellent professional service and consistently good or "high quality" food: rich lobster bisques, creamy soups, perfectly done cuts of meat, masterfully prepared offal and ethereal sauces from seedy mustard to wild mushroom with sauce espagnole.

Like Ayad, Mueller served celebrities like Céline Dion, dignitaries like politicians and ambassadors and even astronauts from the *Challenger* space shuttle.

There was also Le Metro on Elgin Street (which would morph into Metro Café Restaurant before becoming The Manx, arguably Ottawa's first gastropub) and the super chic Le Jardin on York Street.

Thereafter, most of Ottawa's classic French restaurants would close one by one by 2001. They were survived by Laurier Sur Montcalm, which closed in 2004, and Café Henry Burger, which closed two years later.

Chez Jean-Pierre lasted twenty years in its nondescript location beneath a hotel on a side street. Kamal Mehra would open the Ottawa location of East India Company in the space in October 2002. Kamal's son, Nitin, whose formal culinary training comes from both Le Cordon Bleu and Algonquin College, is now chef.

Rise of Canadian Cuisine

The legendary Kurt Waldele, who was born in Buhl, Germany, accepted the executive chef position at the National Arts Centre in 1978. He came to Ottawa by way of Stockholm's Restaurant Opera Alleren, South Africa's Rand International Hotel and Montreal's La Renaissance at Westmount Square Hotel. At the NAC, Waldele would transform food and service, consolidating Le Restaurant into Le Café and creating a focus on Canadian cuisine and expertly crafted dishes, employing the best ingredients from coast to coast. His kitchen attracted culinary talent that would go on to lead the kitchens at Rideau Hall, 24 Sussex and the exclusive Rideau Club. He would promote from within, investing in his staff, who would go on to cook for the British high commissioner and ambassador for the United States.

When he arrived at the NAC, Waldele discovered that fine dining at Le Restaurant involved a salad bar and "harvest buffet." Le Café was a disco, complete with a dance floor and a beer garden. It served hot beef sandwiches and other fast food. Explained Jose Bento, who started as a dishwasher at the NAC in 1978, "With an iron fist, he got rid of canned products. He taught us to make stocks and demi-glace."[9] Bento fondly remembers his former chef swearing about the state of cuisine: "Jesus Christ, what is this?!…You guys don't know how to cook!"

According to Madan Sharma, who started at the NAC in 1994, Waldele would become known for championing Canadian products, even bringing in Canadian wine. "We used to have outdoor 'barbecues' on the terrasse," remembers Sharma. "We would teach people how to grill Canadian salmon and yellow and purple cauliflower." Often, there were 100- to 150-people lineups, so Waldele bought a German sherbet machine and served British Columbia raspberry sherbet in ice cream cones to people in line.

Known for his simple approach to food, featuring the "essence" of Canadian ingredients, Waldele was asked to participate in catering state functions. He served dignitaries from prime ministers to the pope, the queen of England, Princess Diana and President Bill Clinton either in house at the NAC or several blocks away at the National Art Gallery. He was involved in serving delegates who visited Ottawa for Meech Lake deliberations and G7 summits. He was the favourite chef of the Mulroneys, both Brian and Mila.

There were occasions when he would serve 880 kilograms of Matan shrimp for parties at Le Café. His salmon was so popular at an event for Her Right Honourable Kim Campbell that party attendees were grabbing portions straight from the grill. For fundraisers, he was known to steal the show with dishes like smoked salmon filled with crawfish mousse and loin of venison with cranberries and roasted red peppers.

A champion for local culinary talent, he led teams of chefs overseas to compete internationally. Every four years, Waldele would work with the local restaurant industry and Algonquin College to create Ottawa-Hull teams of chefs to compete in the World Culinary Olympics. This involved raising the funds required to travel, purchase ingredients and ship everything overseas.

In 2001, Waldele was team manager of Ottawa's team of chefs that travelled to Glasgow, Scotland, to compete in the ScotHot Competition. The team brought back five gold, two silver and four bronze medals. A grueling forty-eight-hour test of endurance, events involved preparing scores of dishes in a limited amount of time. Ottawa's Marcus Scheiddegger, then of the Westin Hotel, and Clifford Lyness, then of the NAC, took awards. The team brought along Canadian ingredients to showcase, from Quebec squab to poussin (Cornish hen), and served them with root vegetables.

In 2002, Waldele was the team manager of Team Canada, which travelled to Luxembourg, Germany, for the World Culinary Olympics. Competing against nine hundred chefs from thirty-four countries in multiday events that involved preparing hot and cold meals, hundreds of multi-course meals and scores of appetizers and desserts, Team Canada finished sixth, collecting two World Cups and two gold and two silver medals. One of those gold medals was earned by Ottawa's Louis Charest, who worked at Rideau Hall.

When Waldele passed away in 2009, losing his battle with lymphatic cancer, dozens of the National Capital Region's chefs and cooks attended his funeral. He continues to be an inspiration.

Red Tape

Ottawa's food entrepreneurs have run afoul of municipal bylaws and related zoning restrictions for generations. There is very little affecting storefronts, dining rooms or kitchens that isn't regulated, from signage to what can be retailed and even how dishes are prepared. Whether intentional or otherwise, city council helped shape the food scene over the years. In some cases, bylaws redefined how shops and restaurants operated. In others, bylaws invalidated business models, forcing owners to close doors and lay off staff. In designated neighbourhoods, for instance, bylaws prohibited restaurants from erecting large illuminated signs.

Ottawa has a noise curfew (2004-253) that was implemented in 1991. It was deemed draconian by businesses, affecting everything from outdoor loudspeakers to machinery like fans, exhaust systems, furnaces and air conditioners. But one city-driven initiative that changed dining in Ottawa was the smoking ban, forcing diners to butt out!

Dark Clouds of Smoke and Ash

The City of Ottawa, then under Mayor Bob Chiarelli, passed a landmark no-smoking bylaw (2001-148) in 2001. The bylaw did not prohibit smoking outright but rather placed strict restrictions on public spaces, including restaurants, bowling alleys, bars, taverns and bingo and pool halls. Effective August 1, the bylaw was backed by anti-tobacco activists and health officials.

The year before, Dr. Robert Cushman, the region's medical officer of health, pushed the city's then community service committee to fast-track the proposed bylaw. Originally, the restrictions, which built on the province's "Smoke Free" act, targeted restaurants on January 1, 2002, and bars and taverns by 2005. Pre-amalgamation, the Nepean and Kanata municipalities' bylaws had shorter and more aggressive timelines. Theirs were to take effect on May 31, 2001.

Already, restaurants' smoking areas were limited to an ever-shrinking percentage of available floor space, decreasing from 50 percent to 30 percent over ten years. In 1991, Abi-Zeid of Bank Street's former Golden Chalet was the first owner charged and fined ($53.75) for not setting aside half of his ninety-two tables for non-smokers, despite warnings from bylaw officers. Abi-Zeid told the *Ottawa Citizen*'s Elizabeth Payne that he lost thousands of dollars because half of his restaurant was often empty during lunch service, traditionally the busiest time of the day. His regulars used to be federal public servants who could no longer smoke at work.

The new bylaw was even more drastic. It prohibited smoking in common areas of public buildings, public restrooms, food courts, taxis, limousines and public portions of any restaurant or bar. Conspicuous signage was mandated. Proprietors were to remove ashtrays.

Local celebrities Marlen Cowpland and the respected Max Keeping (beloved former news anchor for Ottawa's first television station, CJOH) spoke out about the ban, vowing to take their cigarettes and business across the river into Hull, Quebec. Quebec would see similar no-smoking legislation introduced in 2005.

This wasn't the first competitive advantage given to Hull bars. Many owners likened it to Ontario forcing Ottawa bars to close earlier than their neighboring interprovincial counterpart. Before 1996, last call was 1:00 am. Then, the Mike Harris administration extended it to 2:00 am. For a time, last call meant a mass exodus of patrons from Ottawa into Quebec for at least one more hour of drunken revelry. Hull developed a rather colourful reputation for its busy "after hours" bar strip.

In response, 170 of Ottawa's pub and bar owners formed a coalition, called PUBCO (Pub and Bar Coalition of Ontario), to appeal both the bylaw and fines levied against businesses convicted of violations. One month after the bylaw went into effect, Ontario Superior Court justice Gerald Morin upheld the city's right to establish the bylaw, dismissing the lawsuit launched by PUBCO. PUBCO's appeal of this decision to the Court of Appeal for Ontario would likewise be rejected the following May, in 2002, setting a precedent for the province's other municipalities.

By February 2002, city bylaw officers had issued almost four hundred charges. The former Puzzles Bar in Westboro was fined $360 for permitting smoking and putting out ashtrays. That March, the Newfoundland Pub on Montreal Road was fined $4,500. Then the provincial offenses court ordered Richard Teehen of Cue 'n Cushion to pay $37,895 for repeated violations over the span of about nine months.

Most businesses failed to argue that theirs were exclusive private clubs and so were exempt from the bylaw. At a private club, patrons paid a fee to join and were free to smoke once inside.

With smokers left with no options at bars to drink, PUBCO predicted a collapse in the hospitality industry. However, by 2005, as patrons and staff had become accustomed to the restrictions, restaurateurs started seeing benefits. Owners remarked that their premises no longer reeked of cigarette smoke. Some noticed savings in maintenance, especially cleaning, painting and repairs to air filtration systems. Absenteeism due to illness decreased. Some staff even quit smoking after the bylaw went into effect.

Barbara Mireault of the Fish Market Restaurant in the ByWard Market remarked to Anne Sutherland of the *Gazette* that the ban actually increased turnover amongst smokers, who lingered less in the dining room. While taboo now, it used to be accepted social practice to enjoy a cigarette with your after-meal coffee.

At finer dining restaurants like Preston Street's longstanding Giovanni's, a cigarette was enjoyed with a digestivo (digestif). At the former Le Saint-Ô (327 St. Laurent Boulevard), one of the few classical French restaurants that survived the citywide purge, that digestif was cognac. Explained now retired chef Phillippe Dupuy, who took over Le Saint-Ô in 2000, "After the ban? We lost $25,000 in business, easily!"[10]

A year after the bylaw was put in place, Ottawa councillor Rick Chiarelli issued a press release that a study by city staff showed that eighty-two new bars and restaurants had opened since restrictions were enacted. He further pointed out to Statistics Canada that during the same period, there had only been eighteen bankruptcies in the hospitality sector. Accordingly, there were three more the previous year.

Those restaurants and pubs that survived relied on attracting patrons with creative menus and service. According to PUBCO's Dan Tate, in the twenty months after Ottawa's strict non-smoking bylaws had been put in place, 38 out of 210 bars and pubs closed. Moreover, beer sales (annual orders made to the provincially sanctioned Beer Store by liquor license holders) plummeted 11.5 percent since September 2001. Declines peaked in February and March 2002—17 and 21 percent, respectively.

What Tate does not seem to account for in his statistics involves the general decline in tourism after 2001, due to the emergence of severe acute respiratory syndrome (SARS), the collapse of the local high-tech sector and a weakened American dollar. As for beer sales, Ottawa was in the throes of rediscovering locally crafted beer. Restrictions on smoking on patios followed in 2012.

Chapter 2

WE GROW OUR OWN

Local food is an investment in the future. By supporting local farmers today, you are helping to ensure that there will be farms in your community tomorrow.
—Vern Grubinger, vegetable and berry specialist, University of Vermont

Ottawa is bursting with fine and organic health food shops, various national chain grocery stores, bakeries, coffeehouses, restaurants, fast-food options, pubs, breweries, farmers' markets and businesses dedicated to take-home meal options for people on the go. Everywhere we turn, food is readily available. If it's not in a brick-and-mortar building, it's on television with dedicated twenty-four-hour food channels. Walk into a bookstore, and you'll find shelves brimming with cookbooks of every cuisine known to humankind. These days, it is fashionably hip for people to post their meals on Twitter or Instagram or share endless photos on their Facebook walls. Never have we been more tuned into food than we are now. We are a food-obsessed society.

However, do we truly know where food comes from? Some may say "the farmer," but many, especially the younger generation, will say, "The grocery store!" The more we talk, write, photograph and obsess about food, the more abstract the idea of where food truly comes from becomes. While eating local and shopping at farmers' markets is trendy right now, we have distanced ourselves from how food is grown, where it comes from and how it is prepared.

In the past decade, there has been a strong movement to reclaim our food system, especially in Ottawa. Diners are looking to reconnect with their farmers and growers. There is a renewed emphasis on revitalizing existing farmers' markets and adding new ones in suburbs across the city. The general shopper is becoming more educated at identifying locally grown produce and comparing it to foods purchased from resellers. Community gardens are springing up on empty neighbourhood lots. There are programs in place to help the current and upcoming generations become more involved in the farming process, potentially setting them up to become full-time farmers. Restaurants are partnering with locals farms, featuring their produce and meats on menus.

This is a story of Ottawa reconnecting with its agricultural roots. Settled deep in the Ottawa Valley, the city is home to rich and vast farmland. Agriculture has always been a prominent part of our history. Riverbeds run throughout the valley. Although farms have changed over time, their importance to the area has not.

Heather Hossie, formerly of Just Food, confirmed that Ottawa is in a unique position in that the majority of the city's land mass is rural. In a 2011 census from Statistics Canada, it was found that there were 1,128 farms, with a total of 1,625 operators. The top six farms are dairy, cattle (beef), miscellaneous specialty, vegetable, field crops (excluding grain and oilseed) and grain and oilseed (excluding wheat).

To demonstrate the importance of agriculture to Ottawa, city council put together a report, *The Economic Impacts of Agriculture on the Economy of the New City of Ottawa*, as a basis for describing its rural sector. The findings concluded that Ottawa has the largest agricultural economy of any major Canadian city. With more than $136 million in farm gate sales in 1996, the new city of Ottawa generated more farm revenue than Toronto, Montreal, Vancouver, Edmonton and Calgary combined.

And yet this is only within the city limits. In the areas surrounding Ottawa, the farmland is just as rich, putting the region truly in a class of its own. Hossie proudly states that Ottawa has the most agricultural land of any city in North America: 80 percent rural and 20 percent urban.

Strangely enough, we still have an odd relationship with our food. We've become disconnected with it, as most of our food comes from elsewhere. We've lost touch with knowing what foods are seasonal and when they are best eaten. Generations ago, there was a time when certain foods were available only when in season. In Ottawa, that would be asparagus and strawberries in the spring, tomatoes and zucchini in the summer or apples and squashes in the fall. Nowadays, our ability to ship items all around the world means that many products are pretty much available year-round.

Seasonal and local produce from Rochon Garden in the ByWard Market.

Laurence Cléroux has been selling produce in the ByWard Market for more than fifty years. She feels that we have also become disconnected with our food because we are losing our cooking skills. In recent years, it is not uncommon for buyers to ask how to cook the produce she sells.

As we step back and take time to reeducate ourselves about food, people living in the Ottawa region are most fortunate to have access to farmers' markets throughout the city, bringing fresh, seasonal and most importantly local food.

ByWard Market

Just shy of celebrating 190 years, the ByWard Market in downtown Ottawa is Canada's oldest open-air farmers' market. Established by Colonel John By in 1826 during the construction of the Rideau Canal, the market served as the place where citizens could buy fresh food. Farmers, fish merchants and butchers were crowded together to sell their meats, eggs, fresh vegetables, fruit, fish and even maple syrup. Sardines were bought from barrels, live chickens from cages and fresh bread and tomatoes from bushels.

Soldiers, lumberjacks and labourers tasked with the building of the canal came here to purchase their food. The buggy was the main mode of transportation, and roads were wide. Soon grain and feed stores eventually stood among the general stores, slaughterhouses and fish stalls.

The market itself never expanded beyond its area, still retaining the same boundaries today. However, as Bytown grew from a village to the city of Ottawa and then was named the capital city of Canada, the market became more important. It was always bustling. Farmers came from dozens of kilometres away (and sometimes up to one hundred) to set up stalls to sell their goods.

In the 1970s, the market was still the place where people came to buy all their groceries. Heather Matthews, original owner of Domus, deliberately chose the market when setting up her kitchen store due to the continued vitality of the ByWard Market. She can recall that people lined up at the fish stores and butcher shops on Friday nights when they were open later.

But the 1980s brought significant changes to the market. Since 1847, city government had regulated the market, making decisions that have, at times, proven deeply unpopular. Françoise Cléroux, whose family had been retailing at the market for nearly a century, recalled that her mother used to make blood pudding and headcheese, selling them on wax paper. One day in the mid-1970s, a city official came to her stall and told her that she couldn't sell her homemade products anymore. It was seen as unhygienic.

Up until 1985, live chickens, ducks, geese and goats were still available for purchase. In fact, the ByWard Market was one of the last places in Canada where one could purchase live animals. Philip Powell, who works at City of Ottawa Markets Management, described a typical scene: "People would buy a live chicken, have twine wrapped around the legs and then get on the bus."[11] Unfortunately, a select few who felt squeamish about live animals sold at the market convinced city council to ban them outright. The consequence was a decline in the number of Asian, Italian and Portuguese shoppers coming to the market. In 1995, John Feestra, the last person selling unrefrigerated eggs, was finally driven out by city officials who insisted that he purchase a fridge. Having sold eggs for twenty-seven years, Feestra refused. He no longer has a stall.

However, by the 1990s, the ByWard Market was in serious trouble. First, the market had become a tourist attraction and no longer had the same vibrancy of a true farmers' market. Meat markets became nightclubs, while once beloved local institutions, such as the Zunder family's grocery, became fashion boutiques, souvenir shops and high-end furniture stores. Vendors selling trinkets, clothing and cheap souvenirs replaced longstanding farmer stalls. With the market being located within walking distance of Parliament Hill, museums, the National Art Gallery and the Rideau Canal, tourists would stroll through the ByWard Market. They were less interested in purchasing potatoes and cabbages, favouring instead buying a banana or apple. As the market changed from selling fresh local produce to offering entertainment and tourist attractions, more food shops fell victim to becoming restaurants or non-food retailers.

Second, as people began moving to the suburbs (such as Kanata and Nepean) in the '60s, '70s and '80s, businesses followed them. Eventually, it was no longer necessary for families to come down to the market to make their purchases. As shoppers flocked to grocery stores in the suburbs, they stopped coming downtown. Big-box stores opened, again allowing shoppers to stay in the suburbs to buy flower and vegetable flats and kitchenware. Everything became convenient outside of downtown. This had a devastating effect, particularly for local food vendors. Revenue decreased, and property taxes skyrocketed when the region introduced market value assessment in 1992.

Numerous businesses left, and the face of the market changed. Ritchie's Feed and Seed left. Slover's department store at William and York Streets became Mother Tucker's restaurant (now called Tucker's Marketplace), and the Factory Surplus store at William and George Streets became an Italian restaurant, Oregano's. Today, it is the Grand Pizzeria & Bar. Albert's Meat Market, a fifty-year tenant, also left after owner Daniel Bisson's taxes increased from $15,000 to $75,000 in fifteen years.

Third, and perhaps the most controversial reason, was that the majority of the vendors were not selling produce they had grown. Land-use policy dictated what businesses could operate and where. By 1995, the city was trying to keep a balance between the market staying open seven days a week and ensuring that its vendors still had produce to sell by 5:00 p.m. It would not do if a vendor ran out of locally grown strawberries at noon and had nothing left to sell to customers when they came in the afternoon. Hence, many vendors became resellers or combined locally grown with imported produce. Only a handful of vendors were left selling only what they grew.

In March 1995, the City of Ottawa attempted to regulate the civic markets (this also included the other city's market, Parkdale) by giving incentives and breaks to vendors who only sold what they grew. It was hoped that by doing so, the concept of "farm fresh" goods would ensure the survival of both the ByWard and Parkdale Markets.

Unfortunately, every attempt made by the city failed. Vendors who supplemented their produce with imported products had become very popular, as they could sell their produce cheaper than the vendors who only sold what they grew. Producer-only vendors were furious and strongly lobbied for city council to return it to a real farmers' market. Eventually, the vendors who supplemented took Ottawa's regulatory bylaw to court in the summer of 1995 and had it quashed. The courts considered the bylaw discriminatory, thus throwing it out.

In spite of its struggles, major changes to help shoppers distinguish between vendors who supplemented and those who didn't would eventually come about, but not until well into the 2000s with the creation of Savour Ottawa.

ByWard Market in the Twenty-first Century

In 2014, the ByWard Market continues to be Ottawa's top tourist attraction, a destination for shopping, dining, arts and entertainment and professional services. According to ByWard's Business Improvement Association, the area can receive upwards of fifty thousand visitors per week.

Philip Powell explained the value of the markets to the city, particularly the ByWard Market. Tourists staying in Ottawa for a week or so will often make two to three visits to the ByWard Market. When celebrities visit the city, they are often spotted hanging out in the market. An assessment was done showing that the ByWard and Parkdale Markets are the most valuable urban real estate in North America. Unlike many markets, both ByWard and Parkdale operate seven days a week during the months from May to October, with the ByWard Market operating through the winter, though limited in the number of stalls. Powell described a typical seasonal ByWard Market day as follows:

> *At 6:00 a.m., the trucks are coming in, and the stands are going up. At 7:00 a.m., vendors are setting up. By 8:00 to 8:30 a.m. people are coming in to eat breakfast and grab a coffee. Retailers are ready to open at 9:00 a.m. Lunch usually starts around noon. The busiest time is at 2:00 p.m. This*

The Byward Market on a summer weekend afternoon. Built in 1826, the market is a popular tourist spot.

The ByWard Market. Early fall is one of the best times to shop at the farmers' market, with produce from the late summer and fall harvests.

Sprinkled with sugar and cinnamon, BeaverTails tempt tourists and locals throughout the day and night in the ByWard Market.

> *is the peak hour as tourists generally come at this time. Around 4:00 p.m. people are leaving work and heading home. After that comes the nightlife as people come for dinner, drinks and entertainment. There are one hundred establishments with twenty thousand licensed seats. By 2:00 a.m. the bars are closed and people start heading home. Throughout the evening, there are buskers and people are in line at the BeaverTail stand.*

After almost twenty hours of activity, city crews have between 2:00 a.m. and 6:00 a.m.to clean the streets and replace garbage bins. And at 6:00 a.m., it is the start of a new day as supply trucks roll in.

In 2008, the city made some changes to the market itself, keeping a balance of entertainment (buskers), arts and crafts and agriculture foods. Three categories were set up to help customers distinguish between the food vendors. The first category, farmer, meant that 100 percent of produce sold was grown by the farmer. The second category, farmer-vendor, meant that only 60 percent of produce sold was grown by the farmer. The remaining 40 percent could be supplements. The last category, agri-food vendor, meant that the person was a reseller. To ensure that the category signs posted in the stalls were accurate, inspections by the city were done. This made it easier for shoppers to decide if they wanted to purchase local goods or not.

Parkdale Market

In July 2014, the Parkdale Market celebrated ninety years of service. Located on Parkdale Avenue and Wellington Street West in Hintonburg, it is very much a part of the neighbourhood. However, its history is not without its hiccups. On the first day, two hundred people turned up for the opening ceremonies only for there to be no vendors, as they had all gone straight to the ByWard Market instead. Luckily, the vendors showed up the following week, and customers came back. The Parkdale Market quickly became a success. Within a week of opening, a dozen vendors were in operation. By 1994, there were twenty-five vendors running thirty-nine stalls.

Many of the stalls today are run by the same families, passed from generation to generation. Some of the most recognizable names today include Droun, Rochon, Lacroix, Bergeron, Budd and Cléroux, with Antonio Cléroux being one of the oldest vendors.

Similar to the problems at the ByWard Market, some of the vendors also supplemented with imported produce. With a mix of resellers and vendors who sold only what they grew, shoppers here also had difficulty distinguishing the differences. As the city was unsuccessful regulating the ByWard Market, there was little it could do with Parkdale Market.

Savour Ottawa

In the spring of 2006, the Ontario government released a report identifying Ottawa as one of five provincial regions prepared to be a culinary destination. Ottawa was named alongside Toronto, Niagara, Muskoka and Prince Edward County. The city already had several culinary assets in place: restaurants, farmers' markets, culinary schools (Le Cordon Bleu and the culinary program at Algonquin College) and the Canada Agriculture and

Food Museum. It would not be long before Ottawa was ready to market itself as a culinary destination to the local and international media. To prepare, a committee was formed consisting of representatives from Ottawa Tourism, Just Food and two branches from the City of Ottawa: Markets Management and Rural Affairs.

Ottawa Tourism is a not-for-profit, membership-driven organization that works with its members to profile Ottawa and the capital region as a diverse and exciting place to visit. Just Food is a local, nonprofit, community-based organization that works on rural and urban food issues with the city government. It works hard to ensure that Ottawa is "Food Secure," meaning that everyone at any time has physical and economic access to sufficient, safe and nutritious food in order to meet their dietary needs. This also includes culturally acceptable food preferences. Foods are produced as locally as possible, with production and distribution being socially, economically and environmentally just. Established in 2006, the Rural Affairs branch from the City of Ottawa aims to provide a rural perspective on issues affecting the city, working with rural residents and community groups, city staff and city council to ensure that rural concerns are identified and understood. Finally, the Markets Management Office from the city is responsible for both the ByWard and Parkdale Markets.

With these four groups forming the committee, the vision to promote Ottawa's culinary potential was set. By November of the same year, the first networking summit between chefs, restaurateurs, farmers and culinary institutes was held. Described as a speed-dating event by Jantine Van Kregten of Ottawa Tourism, she emphasized that this face-to-face meeting was a success, as the farmers and chefs came to a greater understanding regarding distribution of local produce, meats and cheeses. Chefs came to know what the farmers grew. Farmers came to an understanding of what crops the chefs wanted to use.

The name Savour Ottawa (*Savourez Ottawa* in French) was coined in 2007 and was officially adopted in 2008. The centre of the corresponding logo features Parliament Hill and a tractor on a field. This represents the unique mix of the urban and rural lands for which Ottawa is known.

The regions Savour Ottawa considers local include Eastern Ontario and western Quebec, as the city sits along the Ottawa River. It aims to promote buying local and eating local. To help people gain a greater understanding and have an easier time identifying local food, farmers, restaurants and food businesses can become members of Savour Ottawa. Each must undergo great scrutiny, as there are various criteria that must

Jantine Van Kregten, of Ottawa Tourism and Savour Ottawa, attends Harvest Table with Chef Charles Part of Les Fougère to help promote eating locally.

Ottawa has the perfect climate to grow mushrooms. These mushrooms are from Champigons le Coprin farm, a member of Savour Ottawa.

be met. Farmers will be verified through the Farmers' Markets Ontario (FMO) MyPick Verified Local Farmer program. This means that local farmers sell only what they grow, raise or otherwise produce on their farms. Restaurants become members if they purchase 15 percent of their ingredients from Savour Ottawa farmers. This is verified by pulling up receipts and examining the charges. For hotel restaurants, this is trickier, and these businesses generally require more food than restaurants. Therefore, hotel restaurants have the option of ensuring that 15 percent or $25,000 worth of ingredients is purchased from Savour Ottawa farmers. Retailers have the option of a minimum purchase of 10 percent annual food purchases sourced from Savour Ottawa producers, a minimum purchase of $25,000 (or $250,000 if it is a large business) annually and directly from Savour Ottawa producers or purchasing from a minimum of ten to fifteen Savour Ottawa producers.

Once farmers, retailers and restaurants meet approval, they gain access to business opportunities. More importantly, they can display a Savour Ottawa sign in their window or stand so that people will know that they are purchasing or consuming local foods.

As both the ByWard and Parkdale Markets have a mix of resellers and vendors with only local goods, shoppers can now look for the Savour Ottawa logo. While this does not completely quash criticism that the markets should go back to their roots, shoppers can now make informed choices.

After one year, Savour Ottawa celebrated its success with close to eighty-five farm and thirty-five restaurant members. Today, Savour Ottawa includes microprocessors as members. Their products are certified individually. These members have the option of ensuring that the first ingredient on the label is purchased directly from Savour Ottawa producer(s) or that a minimum of 51 percent of the product by weight prior to processing is purchased from Savour Ottawa producer(s).

To further promote the farmers to local residents, Savour Ottawa created "trading cards." Similar to sports cards, the front displays a picture of the farmer at his or her farm. The name, location and the distance from downtown are all included. There is also a short introduction, or rather a small summary of the history of the farmer and his or her farm. With these cards on display at the stalls, consumers could collect the trading cards.

Ottawa Farmers' Market

Surprisingly, the Ottawa Farmers' Market (OFM) is a relative newcomer on the food scene. Perhaps, with the long history of the ByWard and Parkdale Markets and the successful launch of Carp Farmers' Market in 1989 out in Carp (forty kilometres west of downtown Ottawa), it was thought that there were plenty of markets residents could visit.

By 1990, new markets had been added in the Ottawa region, including at Almonte, Carp, Kanata and Orleans, joining older, well-established markets. New farmers' markets opened later that year in smaller towns west of Ottawa. This growth was due in part to a four-year-old Ontario government program aimed at encouraging farmers' markets. Robert Chorney, then the Ministry of Agriculture's market development specialist, was hoping that the explosion of farmers' markets would help revitalize ailing downtown areas and towns to feel like a community again. With 60 markets in southern Ontario alone in 1989, there were 90 one year later. Chorney projected that the number would climb to 140 by 1993.

Firmly believing that consumers wanted access to products directly and that farmers wanted access to consumers directly, he figured that everyone would win. As people became concerned about their environmental footprint (excess packaging, long-distance transportation and energy consumption), the demand to experience the true taste of seasonal and locally grown produce and finished products—such as pies and baked goods, without preservatives or additives—grew stronger.

While the Carp Farmers' Market was successful (it celebrated its twenty-fifth season in 2014), markets in Kanata and Orleans disappeared from the community. It would take many years for farmers' markets to appear again in these two suburbs.

By the early 2000s, the demand for a new kind of farmers' market grew. Savour Ottawa did not yet exist, and consumers were becoming frustrated in having to differentiate between resellers and vendors who only sold what they grew. Shoppers were now better educated food-wise and eager to embrace the concept of buy local, eat local. Consumers were reevaluating their relationship with food and looking for fresh, whole products. They wanted to meet the farmers and buy directly from them. From the fields straight to their plates, the old concept of "farm to table" became new again.

A group of dedicated farmers got together to form the Ottawa Farmers' Market. They used the model of the Carp Farmers' Market as their inspiration. Unlike the ByWard and Parkdale Markets, the one in Carp had a very different mandate. Armed with research from the Ontario Ministry of Food and Agriculture, Hildegarde Anderson—with the help of her friend Kathy Fischer and Farmers' Markets Ontario's marketing specialist, Robert Chorney—developed a written plan and conducted a series of information meetings, along with a publicity campaign, to convince members of the community about the potential benefits of a farmers' market. The concept of a producer-based country market was enthusiastically embraced by the community and the Carp Agricultural Society. A nine-member steering committee was formed, with a mandate that all products sold at the market must be grown, raised, produced or manufactured by the vendors themselves. Buying and reselling was not allowed. Anderson's belief in this was so strong that it became the standard for the market.

When the Carp market opened, a crowd of 1,000 customers greeted the vendors. According to the market's website, within one month, the promise of "exceptional produce and craftsmanship" drew in a crowd of 3,500 people. It has become a tremendous success. It also proudly claims on its website that the Carp Farmers' Market is the largest producer-based farmers' market in Eastern Ontario; it is happy to be used as a model for other Ontario markets.

Armed with this information, farmers Andy Terauds of Acorn Creek Garden Farm and Gerry Rochon of Rochon Garden formed a committee along with several of their fellow farmers. Terauds, already selling at Carp Farmers' Market, was interested in catering only to locals. Similar to the sentiment of his colleagues, both men felt that the city's handling of the ByWard Market had destroyed local farmers.

The timing was also right. Back in November 2005, the City of Ottawa held its first rural summit to address the results of the city's 2004 Citizen Satisfaction Survey. It identified that the city's rural residents were significantly less satisfied with municipal services than urban residents. As the result of the two-day summit, many improvements and new initiatives were created for rural Ottawa, including an established City-Centre Farmers' Market. It would be a two-year pilot project. The City of Ottawa also established a Buy Local campaign for its local agricultural products by creating and promoting the Savour Ottawa brand, thus helping urban residents to find and buy locally grown food.

With the city's support of a new farmers' market, finding a suitable location was crucial. First, the location had to be central, meaning both residents and farmers would be able to travel there easily, but it also had to allow for local foot traffic. The location also had to allow room for growth; ample parking was required, and it would preferably be indoors. Having an indoor farmers' market meant that it could be year-round rather than have a May-to-October season. Despite the lack of indoor space, the city decided that the new Ottawa Farmers' Market would be held at Lansdowne Park in the heart of the Glebe neighbourhood.

Another important factor in the creation of the new market was ensuring that shoppers would have excellent choice and selection of local products. They would also be able to buy directly and chat with the farmer. Establishing a relationship between farmer and consumer would likely result in the consumer coming back.

It was also decided that the Ottawa Farmers' Market Association would manage the market itself. The board of directors would have ten members, consisting of a president, vice-president, treasurer, secretary and six directors. It is only fitting that founders of OFM, including Terauds and Rochon, hold the positions of president and vice-president, respectively, with the rest filling in the remaining positions. Ten committees were also formed to oversee various aspects such as finances,

The Ottawa Farmers' Market at its original location before moving temporarily to Brewer Park. In the winter of 2015, the market will return to Lansdowne Park.

membership, a jury, publicity, location, a food court, human resources, a vendor's handbook, education and a committee overseeing bylaws, rules and regulations at Lansdowne Park. Each committee would operate with a chair and fellow members.

Eligibility for membership was strict. With the producers-only concept, members could only sell what they produced. There was zero tolerance for resellers from other public or farmers' markets. Members also had to grow or produce goods within one hundred kilometres of the city of Ottawa, although exceptions would be made at the discretion of the board of directors. An example of an exception would be peaches. As peaches can only be grown in southern Ontario, peach farmers received permission to sell the fruit at the market. Agricultural vendors, arts and crafts, those selling prepared foods and food court vendors were also regulated.

On July 2, 2006, the Ottawa Farmers' Market opened to the public for the first time. Until the end of October, it would operate on Sundays from 8:00 a.m. to 4:00 p.m. There were nineteen vendors on opening day, mostly consisting of producers, with some selling meat and a few arts and crafts vendors. Bearbrook Game Meats was the food vendor, selling a hot breakfast

Farmer Dan O'Brien and his wife, Tammy Oakes, of O'Brien Farms. A member of Savour Ottawa, Dan is also a director of the Ottawa Farmers' Market Association.

Beef from O'Brien Farms continues to be in high demand from chefs and consumers.

Rosemary Kralik of Tiraislim Farm raises Tibetan yak, Highland cattle, sheep, goat and the occasional Tamworth pig.

The Ottawa Farmers' Market at Byron Park in Westboro. The smaller and more intimate market has proven to be successful in the neighbourhood.

and its line of sausages and other meat products. By the end of the first season, there were a total of fifty-nine vendors.

Today, the Ottawa Farmers' Market is a success. While it has had to change its location from Lansdowne Park to Brewer Park due to a two-year construction project, the market is scheduled to return to its original home for the 2015 season. It has also expanded to two additional locations: Byron Park in the Westboro neighbourhood on Saturdays and in Orleans on Fridays.

Asked if he has noticed any changes to the people coming to the market, Terauds nodded his head. "When we were at Lansdowne, it drew an older crowd. But here at Brewer Park, younger families are now shopping. Social media has also help draw young people or 'foodies.' They know that this is the place to be and seen at." It probably helps that the current location is set in a park with lots of green space for children to play and for families to have a picnic. As the market moves back to its original home, the OFM must hold on to to its current customer base while also encouraging those in the Glebe to return next year.

Terauds also commented on the change in attitude people have displayed as he chats with his customers. Kale, once a lackluster vegetable, has really made a comeback. "Six or seven years ago, we would be picking kale in October. These last few years, we've been picking in June, as people are demanding for it. There's also been a rise in Asian vegetables such as bok choy."

"People are asking me, 'What's new this year?'" explained Terauds. Many are curious to know what new produce he is offering. "People who grew up eating from the garden know the difference between local and something from far way. Those who bought from Loblaws don't know the difference. But when they start eating locally, it is to support agriculture and to buy local. They soon realize the difference in taste."

More Farmers' Markets

In the last five years, additional urban farmers' markets have sprung up across the city. Although they are not affiliated with the Ottawa Farmers' Market Association, they are still worth mentioning as they meet a growing demand from consumers looking to get back to basics with their food. The Main Farmers' Market services the Old Ottawa East community, with many nearby residents walking to the market to purchase their food.

The Main Farmers' Market in the Old Ottawa East Community. Vendors must grow or produce their products within 160 kilometres of the neighbourhood.

Initially a pilot project, it is enjoying its fifth season. Another recent market is the Kanata Farmers' Market. Also in its fifth season, the market offers residents in this west end suburb access to producer-only products for those not wanting to make the drive into the city.

A FARMER-RESTAURANT PARTNERSHIP

Although Ottawa-area farms have been supplying local restaurants for many years, the majority of restaurants sourced their meats, eggs and fresh produce elsewhere. Terauds himself had been selling to restaurants for twenty years, but it is only more recently that chefs have expressed a serious interest in buying and serving local. From 2006 to 2013, Savour Ottawa hosted the Farmer-Chef Meet and Greet, similar to its first network summit. Still designed as a speed-dating event, local producers and chefs try to land a "date" with one another. And while Terauds admits that it is not easy to land a date, he admits that Ottawa chefs have no problems connecting with area farmers. With many restaurants serving seasonal menus, a partnership with a local farmer makes sense. Chef John Taylor of the celebrated but recently closed Domus restaurant has often been credited as the "godfather" of regional cooking. He began showcasing local produce on his all-Canadian menu long before buying local was "fashionable."

Another restaurant proud of its relationship with its farmers is ZenKitchen. Dave Loan, founder of the award-winning high-end vegan restaurant, makes a point of not only promoting area farmers on his menu but also featuring local craft brewers and Ontario wines on the drinks menu.

Murray Street Kitchen, Wine and Charcuterie (better known as just Murray Street) is also another well-received restaurant that has taken the "farm to table" and local foods concept very seriously. The names of the farms and artisanal food producers adorn the pages of its menu, essentially a "who's who" list. Chef/co-owner Steve Mitton is proud to point out that just about every product or ingredient used is sourced within Ottawa or Ontario. Of course, there are exceptions, such as salt, many spices and coffee that cannot be grown in Ontario. One exceptional ingredient is Cheese Whiz, usually served on a celery stick with the Murray Street Caesar.

More than ever, Ottawans are looking to get back in touch with food. With the growth of farmers' markets and the demand for local and seasonal products, we are discovering the differences in foods grown locally versus food trucked or flown in from another country. With the help of Savour Ottawa, consumers are learning how to shop again and forming relationships with farmers. Partnerships with chefs and farmers are stronger than ever. The future of local food in Ottawa is looking brighter and more hopeful.

Chapter 3

ICONIC LOCAL FOODS

The founding of Ottawa: Ottawa is a sub-arctic lumber-village converted by Royal mandate into a political cock-pit.

—Goldwin Smith

Canada itself doesn't really have its own cuisine. Similar to our American neighbour, ours is a country of immigrants. The earliest cuisines can first trace their roots back to the Aboriginals and then to the English, French and Scottish. In English Canada, traditional cuisine is closely related to British and Scottish cuisine, while French Canada's fare derived mainly from French cuisine and the winter supplies gathered by fur traders. Waves of immigration in the late nineteenth century and throughout the twentieth would eventually influence the Canadian food scene.

Of course, there are some regional distinctions. Travel to the Maritimes for wild blueberries, Atlantic lobster, salmon, oysters and (from Prince Edward Island) potatoes and mussels. Quebec, la belle province, has tourtière, poutine and maple syrup. Grab a fishing pole and head to Lake Ontario for pickerel and relax with some of summer's finest harvests like corn and peaches. Travel west and one will come across Saskatoon berries and Alberta beef. In British Columbia, people along the west coast love their spot prawns, lobster, wild sockeye salmon, oysters and, of course, Nanaimo bars. Game meat is abundant across the country with boar, bison, venison, caribou and rabbit to name a few. Up north, the Aboriginals have lived off the land for centuries, and their cuisine is based on a mix of wild game, foraged food and some farmed agricultural foods.

For a major city, Ottawa is still relatively young compared to its Canadian counterparts. It doesn't quite have the elaborate food scene of large metropolitan centres like Vancouver, Toronto or Montreal. And it most certainly does not have a comparable population. Ottawa is not a city with major seaports, nor is it a city in which immigrants would primarily choose to settle. While politics and scandals have long been a part of the menu, food seems to be an afterthought.

Walk along a busy downtown street. Stop and ask the locals about the foods unique or iconic to their city. What comes to mind? What do they most identify with? Perhaps it's the Obama cookie, a maple leaf–shaped shortbread cookie made famous by then newly elected U.S. president Barack Obama when he purchased it at the Moulin de Provence bakery in the ByWard Market. Making his first presidential visit to Canada in February 2009, his declaration of his love for this country made the cookies an instant hit. To this day, the cookies are purchased enthusiastically by tourists and locals alike.

Another common response is a traditional poutine. Hot, crispy, golden fries smothered in savoury meat gravy, with squeaky cheese curds, often leave a most satisfying feeling. However, this culinary wonder is actually a Quebec invention. And with Quebec just across the river from Ottawa, it is no surprise that poutine is readily available just about anywhere.

But perhaps the most popular and iconic food that locals will mention is the BeaverTail. First sold at the Killaloe Craft and Community Fair in 1978, this deep-fried icon of the Ottawa Valley is as Canadian as the beaver itself. Shaped like a beaver tail and traditionally sprinkled with cinnamon and sugar, this sweet delicacy has been enjoyed by locals since founder Grant Hooker began selling them in the ByWard Market on June 2, 1980. To this day, it is still being served at its original ByWard Market location, often with long lineups in the afternoons and late summer nights. In the winter, it has become a tradition to skate along the Rideau Canal with a BeaverTail in one hand and a cup of hot chocolate in the other.

In some respects, the BeaverTail is no longer just a local pastry but rather a national symbol, as it is sold from coast to coast, from Whistler, British Columbia, to the Halifax waterfront in Nova Scotia. It is even sold in the United States, and there are plans to open a BeaverTail stand soon in Tokyo, Japan.

Traditional poutine served at Poutine Fest 2014. Golden, crispy fries smothered in gravy and squeaky cheese curds make this an all-time favourite food.

There are no signs of slowing down at Poutine Fest at Sparks Street Malls. With long lineups, customers are excited to sample traditional and exotic poutines.

During the Winterlude festival, cold and hungry attendees line up at a BeaverTail stand.

Each winter, thousands skate along the Rideau Canal, the world's largest outdoor skating rink.

However, Ottawa is much more than just a specialty cookie, poutine or BeaverTail. And we are determined to move past these foods. Although the city has a young food scene, there are restaurants and food businesses that have stood the test of time. Some have become favourites of the elite political staffers. Some are places for family celebrations or special occasions, while others are simply for day-to-day eating. And then there are the businesses that have become neighbourhood or city institutions. Often these are family-own and run, passed down through the generations. Theirs are stories to be told. They are integral to the community. And should their doors ever close, they will be greatly missed.

Mamma Teresa

Take, for example, the beloved Italian restaurant Mamma Teresa. One of the longest-standing Italian eateries in the city, Mamma Teresa has gained a reputation as timeless, making it a culinary landmark. Walking in today, framed and signed photographs densely adorn the walls in the front foyer, a visual list of local and international celebrities and politicians Mamma has fed over forty years.

In 1970, ten years after the family of five arrived in Canada, Teresa Boselli and her son Giuliano opened the doors to Mamma Teresa, originally located at 281 Kent Street. Then, Italian cuisine was considered exotic. Hailing from the Parma region of northern Italy, the food reflected Teresa's roots. Giuliano describes his mother's cuisine as "authentic," made from scratch and perfected through experimentation. The tomato and meat sauces, gnocchi, ravioli and cannelloni are her recipes. In fact, Teresa's recipes still grace the menu today. Well received by critics and locals when it opened, Teresa and Giuliano created something special, quickly making it a popular dining-out choice. Families ate there, whether for an ordinary outing or to celebrate a more intimate occasion. The restaurant even attracted politicians, senators, diplomats, foreign dignitaries and prime ministers—the political elite. Visiting actors and singers also graced Mamma's with their presence.

Eventually, Teresa and Giuliano purchased the nineteenth-century-built Mather House at 300 Somerset Street West in 1984 to accommodate their growing restaurant, and it remains there to this day. And although their dishes have been tweaked over the years to satisfy local tastes, patrons have returned time and time again. "People enjoy it and love it,"[12] Giuliano states proudly. "Parents brought their children, and now their children are bringing their children." As time has marched forward, so, too, has the restaurant. Sadly, Teresa passed away in 2003, and after nearly forty years, Giuliano decided to retire and sold the business to two longtime servers, Walter Moreschi and Frank Schimizzi. For longtime patrons, this was welcome news, as they were quite familiar with these two gentlemen. The fall/winter 2001 edition of *Ottawa Profiles of Success* described Moreschi and Schimizzi as "integral to the history of excellence and hospitality here." Moreschi was seventeen years old when he began working at Mamma Teresa in 1983, while Schimizzi was fifteen when he started in 1984. As busboys, they slowly worked their way up to become bartenders, waiters, managers and, finally, owners. Together with their long-serving chef Rinaldo Falsetti, Moreschi and Schimizzi are proud to continue the tradition of excellence that the Bosellis started all those years ago.

Like any well-established, decades-old restaurant, imagine if the walls of Mamma Teresa could talk. Oh the stories and gossip they could tell! There is the old saying, "What happens in Vegas stays in Vegas." This is also true at Mamma Teresa, with discretion being of the utmost importance. Take a closer look at the photographs hung proudly on the wall. There are the recognizable celebrities, such as American singer Tony Bennett, hockey legend Gordie Howe, Canadian singer Bryan Adams and Hollywood actor Donald Sutherland, all of whom have noshed on a plate of pasta or two. But it is portraits of politicians and prime ministers that stand out. They made Mamma's legendary. Hidden away from the prying eyes of the public, this was the place where Canadian history was made. Many important federal policies of the last thirty years of the twentieth century were heatedly debated in the back room over dinner. If there were angry words or bitterness exchanged, Giuliano has never revealed them. Some policies nearly tore the country apart, pitting provinces, premiers, members of Parliament and Canadians against one another.

It is said that Jerry Yanover, then a young Liberal staffer, was walking home from Parliament Hill when he spotted the new restaurant. Deciding to drop in for a meal, he was quickly won over by Teresa's cannelloni. Pleased, he raved about his meal to Liberal senator Joyce Fairbairn. She and her husband began dining there. Soon after, Prime Minister Pierre Trudeau and his wife, Margaret, along with their children, became its latest patrons. From there, Mamma Teresa became a popular destination for members and staff of the federal Liberal Party. To this day, senators and MPs (members of Parliament) of both the Liberal and Conservative Parties continue to frequent Mamma's.

One of the most important pieces of Canadian legislation of the twentieth century, the Constitution Act (1982), will be forever associated with Mamma Teresa. At the time, Prime Minister Trudeau and the Liberal government sought to patriate the Constitution of Canada from the United Kingdom. As the country's original constitution was a British act, the Canadian government had to apply to the British Parliament if it wanted to make any amendments. With the passing of the 1982 act, Canada no longer needed to seek permission from England. While most Canadians associate the birth of the Canadian Charter of Rights and Freedoms with the new act, the controversy lay in the amending formula. In 1981, many provinces, including Quebec, initially resisted the formula, fearing that it would weaken provincial powers. A total of eight provinces stood against Trudeau. Discussions between the provinces and Trudeau went back and forth for several months. By November of that same year, some of the premiers had realized that Trudeau and Quebec premier René Lévesque would never be able to settle their differences. As a result, a few provincial leaders began negotiations with their federal counterparts. Over a plate of cannelloni at Mamma Teresa, journalist Allan Fotheringham reported that Attorney General of Saskatchewan Roy Romanow and Attorney General of Ontario Roy McMurty "stumbled upon one another's appetites and began some calorie-trading…When the country is saved, it will be known as the Pasta Pact." Hailed as a historical evening, local media dubbed the dinner between the attorney generals as the "Cannelloni Accord." A framed copy of the article about the encounter now hangs on the wall of this esteemed eatery.

POLITICAL HANGOUTS

As this is the political capital of Canada, our parliamentarians also have their favourite watering holes. While they may not necessarily be culinary landmarks, the restaurants, pubs and bars are still worth mentioning. These are the places where policies are debated and discussed in a more relaxed manner outside the House of Commons and away from the camera. In 2012, reporter Tristin Hopper wrote for the *National Post* that "people on [Parliament Hill] work incredibly hard—but they drink incredibly hard." From the Conservatives to the Liberals, Bloc Québécois, NDP (New Democratic Party) and Green Party, there is something for them all. For Canadians hoping to catch a glimpse of their MPs, Ottawa is the place to see the action. Within walking distance of Parliament Hill, there are at least forty bars, pubs, restaurants, taverns and nightclubs. This does not include businesses scattered across downtown or just over the bridge into Gatineau.

The Métropolitain Brasserie attracts the political elite with Hill Hour, three hours of late-afternoon cheap oysters and specials. However, it is commonly known as the territory of the Conservatives. At the corner of Sparks and Elgin Streets, D'Arcy McGee's is a favourite with journalists, lobbyists and MPs of all stripes, although it is reported to be mainly Liberal turf. The NDP has adopted the ByWard Market bar Brixton as its permanent hangout. Cock and Lion, also on Sparks Street, is another low-key pub affiliated with the Liberals. The high-end steakhouse Hy's is associated with every party, although mostly with the senior members of the political elite. Similar to Mamma Teresa, Hy's is no stranger to the occasional backroom deal. Another all-party pub on Sparks Street is the Parliament Pub. Here, many dishes on the Hill-themed menu are named after cabinet ministers and well-known MPs. And of course, who can forget Sir John A Pub on Elgin Street? Named after Canada's first prime minister, Sir John A. Macdonald is the only Conservative and prime minister to have led six majority governments. It is only fitting that this is also a favourite watering hole of the Conservatives.

Interestingly, despite the go-to hangouts of the current ruling Conservative government, Hopper noted, "After their 2006 election… the caucus was carefully warned against public intoxication and was said to be banned from entering D'Arcy McGee's outright." The accuracy of this ban is rather debatable, as locals have seen some Conservatives at D'Arcy's. But in a 2012 e-mail exchange between the *National Post* and Ottawa restaurant critic Anne DesBrisay, she wrote, "Conservatives don't seem to have fun anywhere. Never see them." Furthermore, Hopper wrote, "It appears they do their drinking in private receptions at the Métropolitain and Sir John A Pub."

Golden Palace

Over the years, Golden Palace on Carling Avenue has received numerous orders for its most famous and sought-after appetizer. It has been widely reported that sometimes orders are bound for a nearby hospital, where a terminally ill patient wants one last serving of this specialty. Each December, hundreds of orders are prepared and shipped across Canada—from Victoria, British Columbia, to Labrador City, Newfoundland, and as far north as Nunavut. Outside Canada, orders have travelled to the United States, Grand Cayman Island, Bahamas, Bermuda, Switzerland, United Kingdom, Sweden and Amsterdam. Heading west, this little appetizer has travelled all the way to Maui, Hawaii. Story has it that some people order them on Christmas Eve and later place them under the tree to be opened on Christmas morning. It is not unusual for parents to place an order or two, only to box the appetizers up and then send them as a care package to their children. And never mind the expensive and fancy restaurants at which singer Paul Anka could eat. When he comes home to Ottawa for a visit, Anka is at Golden Palace with his bodyguard. Former prime ministers Lester B. Pearson, Pierre Trudeau, Joe Clark and Jean Chrétien have dined here on numerous occasions. Each April, since its fiftieth anniversary in 2010, hundreds if not thousands of people have lined up at dawn to help this Chinese-Canadian restaurant celebrate its milestones.

This treasured and irresistible signature food is none other than the humble open-end egg roll. The work starts before dawn at Golden Palace. Seven days a week, by 4:00 a.m., a small team of ladies begin making the egg rolls by the hundreds. The filling is made of pork, celery, onions, cabbage and bean sprout and then wrapped. The recipe, perfected by Chef Kim Wong's father back in 1940, has a few more ingredients that have remained a trade secret. Manager Yuen-Ping Lee has repeatedly said that there are one or two components he won't reveal for fear of competitors copying the recipe. If there is any anxiety about the ladies giving up the secret, he's not worried, as they are very loyal. Some of the women have worked there for more than forty years. The eldest is in her seventies, while the youngest is in her fifties.

After fifty-four years, Golden Palace is Ottawa's longest continuously running Chinese restaurant, making it a beloved landmark. Today, Bill Kwong is the third-generation owner. Together, he and Lee are overseeing a new generation of diners. In fact, it is not unusual for multiple generations to sit at the same table. Meanwhile, Kwong has found a way to spread the love of the fabled egg rolls to a new audience. In 2012, he secured a deal to offer the egg rolls at Scotiabank Place (now called Canadian Tire Centre), home of the National Hockey League team, the Ottawa Senators. Local television news station CTV Ottawa reported that in its first season, about seventy thousand egg rolls were sold at just the games alone. As it stands today, Golden Palace egg rolls are available not only at the Senator games but also at the Ottawa 67's games, the city's junior hockey team.

To further elevate the tale of the egg rolls, Gary Dimmock, a reporter at the *Ottawa Citizen* newspaper, described it best in his 2009 article:

> *A few years ago, an Ottawa bartender on his way to visit family out west, walked through airport security with some of Golden Palace's finest, only for a security man to ask him what was in the bag. He said egg rolls. The security man quickly asked: "GP?" The bartender said yes, and with that, he was on his way.*

MONTREAL-STYLE BAGELS

They might not be as famous as those in New York City, and there might not be a bagel war similar to the one in Montreal, but Ottawans love their bagels. The two largest bagel businesses, Ottawa Bagel Shop & Deli and Kettleman's Bagel Company, have been satisfying local cravings for Montreal-style bagels for a number of years. What makes Montreal-style bagels so unique? Unlike the New York–style ones, these handmade bagels are smaller, sweeter and denser, with a larger hole. Ingredients include malt and egg (there is no salt), and they are boiled in honey-sweetened water before being baked in a wood-fired oven. The two most popular varieties are white sesame seed and the black poppy seed bagels.

While Ottawa doesn't have a storied and fierce bagel war similar to Montreal's infamous competition between Fairmont and St. Viateur, it is still worth exploring to see who makes the best bagel in the nation's capital.

Founded by Montreal natives Craig Buckley and Joe Bianchini, Kettleman's opened in April 1993 in the heart of the Glebe neighbourhood. Open twenty-four hours a day every day of the year, Kettleman's prides itself on giving customers the best, authentic bagels and a "no-wall"

At Kettleman's Bagel Company, a bagel roller rolls the dough into the familiar shapes.

A wooden board of sesame seed–covered bagels is ready for the wood-burning oven.

experience—meaning that when patrons walk in, they will immediately see bagel rollers rolling and working with fresh dough and cutting it into the proper portions. Regardless of where one stands, just about anyone can see the entire process from start to finish. The shop is always bustling, as the comforting doughy smell hangs in the air. Said Buckley, "I've had lineups at every hour of the day."[13] Other specialties include the kosher dill pickles, a pizza bagel all dressed, the bagel dog, knishes (choice of potato, spinach or pizza) and its famous pretzel. Many Glebe residents will happily argue that the best bagels are right at their doorstep. And they are not the only ones who love them. Asked to share a memorable event, Buckley noted, "After Bluesfest one year, [English singer] Sting came in and bought sandwiches for his crew and left a fifty-dollar tip. Money well spent!"

Meanwhile, other locals will point to the Ottawa Bagel Shop for this city's best bagels. Established in April 1984, the bagel shop is a beloved family business in the Hintonburg and Wellington West neighbourhoods. Founded by Vincenzo Piazza, he also has the honour of bringing the first wood-burning oven to Ontario. Together with the help of his brother-in-law, Joe Morean, owner of Montreal's St. Viateur Bagel, they opened a nine-hundred-square-foot store that carried about twenty-five products alongside the bagels. Although business was slow at first, it did not take long before customers came clamouring for the warm, yeasty-smelling goods. Over the years, the storefront eventually expanded to more than seven thousand square feet and also boasts a successful restaurant, often busy with families having bagel sandwiches and platters for breakfast or lunch. With a few elementary schools nearby, young teenagers are often seen walking into the Bagel Shop for a quick lunch. It is a rather heartwarming sight, seeing a group of friends sitting on the edge of the sidewalk, laughing with drinks in their hands and passing a bag of bagels amongst themselves.

After thirty years, the shop has served millions of bagels. With bagels coming out of the oven every three minutes, that is about six thousand bagels per day, 360 days of the year. In addition, Piazza has one hundred suppliers around the world, bringing unique and exclusive products to his patrons. But he's also an enthusiastic supporter of local artisans, stocking everything from cookies to cupcakes, jams, sauces, chutneys and mustards from Mrs. McGarrigle's.

These days, although customers can still find Piazza in the shop, he is handing over the family business to his daughter, Liliane.

BRIDGEHEAD

When Bridgehead opened its flagship coffeehouse on June 17, 2000, at 362 Richmond Road in the Westboro neighbourhood, it was a resounding success. Within a few years, Bridgehead was voted by readers of the weekly lifestyle *Ottawa XPress* as the city's "Best Coffee/Tea House." Over the years, the business has since expanded to multiple locations. Operating exclusively in Ottawa, many locals will be surprised to learn that this beloved coffee chain did not actually start here, but rather in Toronto.

Founded in 1981 by two United Church ministers and two social activists, Bridgehead Trading was formed as a result of concerns for the prospects of small-scale coffee farmers in Nicaragua. As the company website notes, farmers were faced with many hardships, including trading through a third-party, civil war and restrictions from a U.S. trade embargo. As a result, Bridgehead became the first Canadian company to offer fairly traded coffee to the public. From a Toronto church basement, a group of dedicated volunteers began selling coffee to a growing number of interested patrons. The company was so well received that within three years, Bridgehead had outgrown its space and voluntary management.

Obtained by Oxfam Canada in 1984, Bridgehead became a federal, for-profit company. Unfortunately, decisions to diversify the product line to include artisan handicrafts proved to be its downfall, going from profit to losses. New ownership by U.K. cooperative lending society Shared Interest in 1998 eventually returned Bridgehead back to its grassroots, a fairly traded coffee and tea company.

By the end of the 1990s, the Ottawa java landscape comprised mainly American coffee giant Starbucks and three Canadian chains: Second Cup, Tim Hortons and Timothy's World Coffee. When local entrepreneur Tracey Clark bought the Bridgehead Trading Company, Ottawans were eager to embrace fairly traded coffee and tea. After the opening of her first coffeehouse, she has since expanded, concentrating mainly in downtown, with a handful in the suburbs of Glebe, Westboro, Hintonburg and West Wellington Village.

Today, there are fifteen locations and counting, including its own roastery, which opened in June 2012. Located in the Little Italy neighbourhood, Bridgehead now roasts all of its coffee beans in-house. While there are plans to expand beyond Ottawa in the future, Bridgehead remains very much a beloved chain for locals looking to get their caffeine fix. Although Clarke did not specify the neighbourhood, the *Ottawa Business Journal* printed an excerpt from her book *That'll Never Work*, and her description of one particular expansion proved just how important Bridgehead had become: "[T]here was another location in Ottawa that came to our attention… Oddly enough, we were competing with Starbucks, and the residents from the neighbourhood actually presented a petition to the landlord saying they would prefer a Bridgehead. The landlord gave the location to us and the timing was perfect."

PHO AND SHAWARMA HOUSES

Given the large communities of ethnic Vietnamese and Lebanese people living in Ottawa, it is not surprising to see the number of pho and shawarma houses. Political unrest and conflict are often reasons why people immigrate to Canada. And with them, they bring their culture, traditions and foods. The 1982 civil war in Lebanon and the formation of communist governments in Vietnam, Cambodia and Laos in 1975 forced millions of people to flee. Many eventually settled in Ottawa.

Along the one-kilometre stretch of Chinatown, there are more than a dozen Vietnamese restaurants, with the majority of them being pho noodle houses. Today, there are pho noodle houses in every suburb in the city. Meanwhile, with Ottawa having the country's highest percentage of Lebanese restaurants, there is a shawarma shop on every other corner in the downtown core, sometimes multiple locations within a city block. A few years ago, in *National Geographic*'s travel section, a list of the "Top 10 Foods to Eat in Ontario" was put together. Shawarma in Ottawa was ranked number six. Perhaps Ottawa really is the shawarma capital of Canada!

Whether platters served with pita or pita-wrapped sandwiches, "shawarma" here is defined as consisting of shaved vertical rotisseried meat (chicken or beef), optionally served with shredded lettuce, tomato, pickled turnips and thick garlic sauce ("toum"). Platters tend to include rice and potatoes.

Numerous longstanding restaurants and businesses continue to be greatly cherished by locals. However, an emerging generation of cooks, chefs, bakers and artisanal food producers are lovingly capturing the unique tastes and flavours this region has to offer.

Rise of Local Artisanal Foods

With a rich farming history and long-established farmers' markets, Ottawa has always had artisanal producers. However, as the world changed, so, too, did the shopping habits of most Canadians. We slowly moved away from shopping and eating locally and bought groceries at the supermarkets. In recent years, our increasing demand for locally grown produce also fueled the desire for locally made products. This resulted in a renewed focus on artisan food, delicious products made in small batches by hand and with heart. While it is impossible to name them all, there is a group that has set itself apart. Many of these producers have become major vendors at farmers' markets. Fine food shops stock their products. Some have even gone on to open their own restaurants.

Art-Is-In Bakery: With a number of longstanding bakeries in town, there was heavy competition for customers. However, one chef managed to capture the attention of bread lovers at a time when the gluten-free diet was emerging as the newest fad. No stranger to the restaurant industry, Kevin Mathieson was enticed to come to Ottawa back in 2003 by then executive chef Michael Blackie. Hired on the spot, he became the pastry chef at Perspectives restaurant at the Brookstreet Hotel. He also later worked as the pastry chef for former prime minister Paul Martin. But his passion for making breads and pursuing his dream of opening his own business could not be ignored. With the support of Robert Bourassa, owner of former Café Henry Burger, and Vincenzo Piazza of Ottawa Bagel Shop, Mathieson established Art-Is-In Bakery. Originating as a satellite bakery in a space behind the bagel shop, Art-Is-In began supplying breads to many of the city's top restaurants. Using artisanal baking techniques, the recipes he developed for his unique line of breads set him apart. Recognizable across Ottawa, loaves of Art-Is-In breads were soon available for purchase at various food shops and at farmers' markets. By 2010, this one-of-a-kind bakery found its new home at the City Centre (250 City Centre Avenue), where eager customers line up to purchase Mathieson's breads, sandwiches, French pastries and baked goods. Also a restaurant with brunch and lunch services, it has been named as one of Ottawa's top restaurants since 2012.

Kichesippi Beer Co.: A family-owned business, founders Paul Meek and his wife, Kelly, are determined to create a beer exclusive to Ottawa. Bursting onto the craft beer scene in mid-2010, Kichesippi beers are poured and served in restaurants, pubs and taverns across the city. With the beers

While the Kichesippi Beer bike isn't used for delivery, it is attached to a great keg of beer.

being crafted off Carling Avenue, Meek gets straight to the point: "We love being part of the local experience. We're trying to be a part of that identity, to be something that Ottawa can be proud of." As of 2013, Meek began producing a new line of beverage at the brewery, Harvey and Vern's sodas. Described as an old-fashioned soda due to the drinks being sweetened with cane sugar, it also does not contain sodium benzoate preservative nor artificial colouring. The first flavours were ginger beer and cream soda. Root beer soon followed. The name pays homage to Meek's grandfather (Harvey) and his father-in-law (Vern).

MICHAELSDOLCE: Since the summer of 2009, former pastry chef Michael Sunderland began devoting his passion for food into artisanal jams, fully establishing his brand michaelsdolce by January of the following year. As a member of Savour Ottawa, what makes Sunderland's jams unique is his ability to capture the fruits and flavours of Ottawa in every jar. Ingredients not native to the region—such as oranges, lavender, peaches and star anise—are often paired with local and seasonal fruits like strawberries, wild blueberries, cranberries and rhubarb. Nearby farms he has paired with include Rochon Gardens, Upper Canada Cranberries, Millers Farm

Michael Sunderland, creator of michaelsdolce jams, is one of Ottawa's best-known jam makers.

Pascale Berthiaume's popsicles are another favourite at the Ottawa Farmers' Market. Her delightfully rich ice cream is considered a local gem.

Chef/Owner Marysol Foucault of Edgar would like to see Ottawa develop its own food identity and take pride in it.

and Warrner's Farm from Beamsville, Ontario. As for the jams themselves, they are not cloyingly sweet. And with a variety of textures, these creations are true to the fruit they are made with. The smells, look and colour all scream of fruit. Each flavour-paired jam is custom. With the ingredient list varying from jar to jar, everything is meant to complement the fruit. Sold at the Ottawa Farmers' Market and various food shops across the Ottawa and Toronto regions, shoppers can find more than a dozen varieties, including chocolate raspberry jam using local artisanal chocolate maker Hummingbird and, his latest offering, peach and sriracha jam, made with his own sriracha sauce.

PASCALE'S ALL NATURAL ICE CREAM: Pascale Berthiaume became famous for her ice creams when she was the pastry chef at Wellington Gastropub. By 2009, she had left the restaurant and started her own business, Pascale's All Natural Ice Cream, selling half-pints of her frozen creamy delights at the Piggy Market in the Westboro neighbourhood. An image of her smiling face makes her brand instantly recognizable. Her ice cream has since come to be regarded by many as a local gem. Made from the heart, Pascale uses a French custard base to thicken her ice creams—lots of full-fat cream from Cochrane's Dairy, sugar and egg yolks. Any vanilla used is scraped directly from the pod, and only whole fruit is employed. The same year she went into business, *Ottawa Magazine* listed Pascale's ice cream on the "101 Must-Try-Before-You-Die Tastes" list, ranking it at number two. Today, with nearly thirty flavours, some of her signature ice creams include French vanilla, peanut butter salted caramel, malted milk chocolate, dark chocolate sea salt and milk chocolate Beau's Beer. There are also a few vegan choices and seasonal flavours, such as egg nog and honey rhubarb ginger. There is even goat cheese ice cream for those looking for something more adventurous.

With many iconic and beloved foods and businesses, the quest for great local food is only beginning. As Chef/Owner Marysol Foucault of Edgar explained, "We're a very young food scene. Ottawa still needs to find an identity. We're always trying and chasing the newest food trend. Why can't we be a city that's a freaking master of something?"[14] As the city marches onward, our chefs and food and drink producers have much to offer.

Chapter 4

DINING OUT IN THE NATION'S CAPITAL

Four people walk into the ByWard Market on a warm, sunny Friday evening: a senior communications analyst, an ethics officer, a political aide and an administrative assistant. They stop to decide where to grab dinner. After a lengthy discussion, referencing several online review sites for guidance (Yelp, Urbanspoon and Ottawa Foodies), one exclaims in exasperation to the others, "Why isn't there a good place to eat in the market?"

It is 2014. How can this be? According to Tripadvisor, Ottawa now has more than two thousand restaurants, many of them concentrated in the entertainment and tourism district that has become the ByWard Market.

A Tour of the ByWard Market

At the higher end (thirty-five to forty dollars for an entrée and fifteen to twenty dollars for an appetizer), there is the Empire Grill (47 Clarence Street), now a reinvented "Italian-inspired" steakhouse inside the Time Square Building. During Ottawa's short-lived rise to become Silicon Valley North, Gary Thompson, John Borsten, David Leith and David Mangano opened the 230-seater bar and grill at the corner of Clarence Street and Parent Avenue, intending it to offer the newly affluent a 1940s New York–

style vibe. Thompson used to work in insurance. Originally the Sunset Grill California Food Emporium, the location was collateral on a loan that Thompson made to another restaurateur. When his client defaulted and Thompson was unable to find a buyer to cover his losses, he partnered with Mangano, Borsten and Leith to open Empire in February 1998.

The steakhouse introduced downtown Ottawa to a modern, high-end dining experience with a twelve-metre cherry wood bar and a one-thousand-square-foot patio. Empire is strategically located in a prime tourist location, central with foot traffic. It specializes in meat (hand-cut thirty-five-day aged angus steaks) and martini cocktails. Borsten, Mangano and Leith learned the restaurant business, starting as busboys. Borsten started at former GuadalaHarry's on York Street (18). He then opened the now Firestone property Blue Cactus (Tex-Mex with slushy drinks) in 1989 and bought venerable faux-retro Zak's Diner (swivel chairs, checkerboard tiles, chrome accents and diner fare), opening other locations in the Glebe (now closed) and Kanata. Mangano and Leith started at former Peppers on Elgin. Among other pub and café properties, Mangano and Leith opened Fresco Bistro Italiano on Elgin (354), which survives today with a sister restaurant in the west end suburb of Kanata.

Thompson, Borsten and Mangano would go on to open the stylish, French-inspired Metropolitain Brasserie at the bottom of a very swanky condo building in March 2005, just beyond the borders of the ByWard Market on Sussex Drive (700). A "taste of twentieth-century Paris," the 6,700-square-foot space with 260 seats features zinc counter tops and artificially worn surfaces, costing $1.8 million in renovations. Outside, the sunken courtyard seats another 60. Initially, Metropolitain served contemporary twists on French fare conceptualized by Chef John Taylor of former Domus Café (85 Murray Street): salad niçoise, eggs cocotte and whole roasted chicken. The current menu includes steak frites (Angus rib-eye with Golden Arches–inspired shoestring fries), coq au vin (with chicken supreme), beef short rib bourguignon, cheeseburgers, lobster mac 'n' cheese and spaghetti carbonara (with wild boar bacon lardons, peas, pecorino Romano and cracked black pepper). These days, the Metropolitain is known very well to the political crowd for its "Hill Hour" specials and raw bar.

In 2009, Thompson, Borsten and Mangano replaced longtime ByWard Market pasta eatery Oregano's with a wood-fired pizza restaurant called the Grand (74 George Street). Dating back to 1882, the brick building started life as the Grand Hotel. Marketing it as an authentic Napoletana pizzeria, they even brought in a chef from Naples, for a time, to ensure that the pizzas conformed to the standards of Italy's Associazione Verace Pizza Napoletana. In 2013, they replicated their French brasserie concept at the corner of Richmond Road and Churchill Avenue, former home of Moe Atallah's World Famous Newport Restaurant (a Colonnade Pizzeria analogue), investing $1 million. Called Savoy Brasserie (334 Richmond Road), it has become known for its "Westboro Hour" specials and raw bar. In 2014, they replicated the Italian pizzeria concept in the southwest suburb of Barrhaven, opening Angelucci's (3101 Strandherd Drive) in March. The enormous restaurant sports an expanded menu of reputedly southern Italian fare. It has a "Barr Hour."

At the lower end (thirty dollars for fajitas for two), there is Lone Star Texas Grill (128 George Street). Originally the Lone Star Café, the successful chain of restaurants features mesquite smoke–flavoured Tex-Mex fare, young servers who use quirky cowboy names and eager southern hospitality. It launched its first location at the corner of Baseline Road and Fisher Avenue in 1986. Eight years later, there would be eleven Lone Star locations from Ontario to Nova Scotia. The original, with its 144-seat dining room and an 80-seat patio, was opened by former Canadian Football League (CFL) players Val Belcher and Larry Brune and former general manager Jake Dunlap. Located in a once sleepy suburban strip mall, it broke records, attracting about five to six thousand people every week, which translated into turning seats three to six times a night. There were lineups.

Belcher, who led the Lone Star Group of Companies that operated Lone Star Texas Grill and Big Daddy's Crab Shack and Oyster Bar until 2003, first tackled the food world when he and his wife, Terri, started a sandwich stand in 1981 at Lansdowne Park, home of the former Ottawa Rough Riders. The Houston native played at Frank Clair Stadium. She served "Belcher Burgers" tailgate style, and they became a game day staple: thin strips of mesquite- or hickory-smoked beef brisket and family secret recipe barbecue sauce on a soft burger bun. For Lone Star, Belcher and Brune wanted to share the home cookin' they grew up with in a laidback, casual atmosphere. They built Lone Star's menu around fajitas: grilled skirt steak or chicken breast on house-made flour tortillas. Belcher would go on to open Big Easy's Seafood & Steak House on Preston Street. He passed away in 2010.

Belcher's son, Layne, would carry on the family legacy, opening the "New Street Food Vendor Program" incumbent Urban Cowboy food truck in 2013. On his menu is the Belcher Burger, now served on a potato bun, made with potatoes from a North Gower farm. With the return of CFL football to Ottawa the following year, Layne served his family's burger at a tailgate party in a beer garden next to the Aberdeen Pavilion at Lansdowne Park on opening night. The new team, the Ottawa RedBlacks, went on to win that night's game against the Toronto Argonauts.

Then there are the wondrous, independently owned, chef- or restaurateur-led (but chef-driven) small restaurants that seem to make up a growing culinary underground, depending on your exposure to Ottawa's food scene. For the longest time, visitors to the ByWard Market's main strip along York Street saw only its three side-by-side big-box restaurants: Tucker's Marketplace (a venerable buffet house that was once called Mother Tucker's), the former Hard Rock Café and The Keg. Look harder.

There are restaurants where the kitchen is made up of a traditional brigade system and where food is produced by heavily skilled hands. At the opposite end of York Street, the end that butts up to Sussex Drive, there is Carolyn Gosselin's Restaurant E18hteen and Sidedoor Contemporary Kitchen and Bar. Opened in 2001, 120-seat E18hteen was always meant to be a splurge, a special-occasion restaurant to celebrate life's triumphs. One of the highest-end restaurants in the city, E18hteen became recognized for trendy Asian-inspired food when Chef John Leung returned to Ottawa after running the kitchen at Boston's Aujourd'hui Restaurant in the Four Seasons Hotel. Gosselin hired him to leverage the expertise he picked up at Nobu and Sugar in London, England. A rite-of-passage kitchen, former chefs Chris Deraiche of the Wellington Gastropub and Matt Carmichael of El Camino passed through its doors. Its most recent departure, Chef Walid El-Tawel, earned E18hteen four CAA/AAA diamonds, a coveted recognition of consistent quality in dining and service.

Opened in 2011, Sidedoor is helmed by former *Top Chef Canada* finalist Jonny Korecki. His kitchen is equipped with well-worn wooden and stone mortars and pestles, each dedicated to specific dishes. His is a kitchen of cleavers and handcrafted Japanese carbon steel knives that produces rather authentic Asian dishes and two crowd favourite staples: tacos and doughnuts. It is a poorly kept secret that Sidedoor prepares Momofuku-style ramen noodles from scratch during lunch service. Momofuku is a chain of restaurants launched by New York Chef David Chang, who innovated a method for making ramen noodles using sodium carbonate instead of lye water.

On Murray Street, there is Navarra Restaurant (93). Locally trained chef René Rodriguez's six-year-old Navarra was often overlooked when journalists compiled "top ten" restaurant lists for the nation's capital. That is, until Rodriguez took the *Top Chef Canada* title for 2014—the last title, as

Chef Jonny Korecki at Ottawa's first Noodlefest, plating up bowls of entirely scratch-made ramen.

the Food Network has chosen to no longer produce the competition. Serving finer dining takes on Oaxacan (Mexican) cuisine with Roman and Basque (Spanish) influences, meals at Navarra are always rich and flavourful. Dishes are plated with extreme attention to detail, an intricate feast for the eyes and palate. Think braised pig cheek with manchego, ibérico chorizo– and potato-stuffed ancho chiles rellenos, beef tartare with pistachio romesco and chives and rabbit confit "chilaquiles" with Serrano chili-tomato salsa.

Across the street is Murray Street Kitchen, Wine and Charcuterie (110 Murray Street). Ottawa is home to 1,128 farms. Farm-to-table may be a fad in other cities, but it isn't here, especially after Chef Steve Mitton and Paddy Whelan opened Murray Street Kitchen in 2008. Both formerly of Peter Boole's Social, they exposed the city to its first charcuterie bar. Serving Canadian contemporary comfort with Austrian and German influences, Murray Street has a strong "local" ethic. The menu constantly changes to accommodate available meat and produce. Soul-satisfying plates are whimsically named, oftentimes after farmers. Think pork cretons, gnocchi in smoked lamb bolognese and duck fat poached beef short rib. In 2009, Air Canada's *En Route* magazine listed Murray Street Kitchen as one of Canada's "Best New Restaurants." Even John Cattuci of Food Network

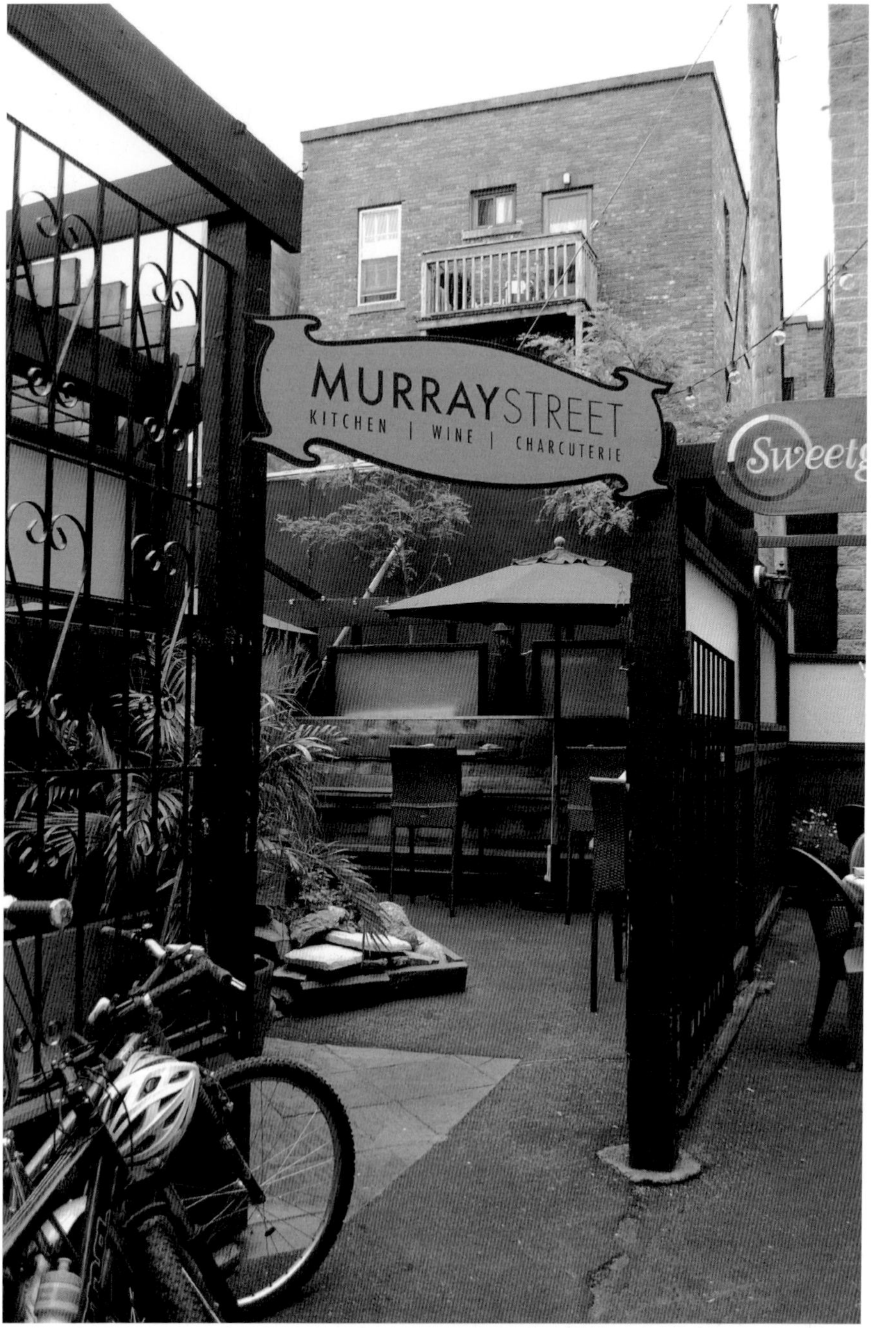

Murray Street Kitchen, Wine and Charcuterie's urban oasis of a back patio.

Canada's national travel program *You Gotta Eat Here* stopped by in 2012 to film a segment.

On Sussex Drive, there is Social. Taking over the rite-of-passage kitchen from Jordan Holley, who now leads El Camino's kitchen on Elgin Street, Chef Kyrn Stein has been working to rebrand the restaurant to attract young professionals to come for drinks but stay for dinner. Since October 2013, he has brought in Ontario lamb; Organic Oceans steelhead trout from Lois Lake, British Columbia; and organic produce from Juniper Farm in Wakefield, Quebec. The intent is to showcase Canada's best agricultural products from "pork to chickpeas." Stein brings with him an impressive résumé, representing almost a decade of cooking in professional kitchens. Besides staging at Pied à Terre, a Michelin starred French restaurant, in London, England, Stein worked his way around a number of Toronto's notables. His employers include the McEwan Group and Jamie Kennedy. However, it was his time spent at Claudio Aprile's former Colborne Lane and Ben Heaton's The Grove that would define his approach to fine dining, especially his intricate and thoughtful plating. One of his more impressive dishes from his winter menu was vadouvan lamb saddle with belly daal, cauliflower and poppadum yogurt. On his newly launched summer menu, the lamb saddle is now served with artichoke, minted potatoes, white anchovies and Cumberland sauce.

On Dalhousie Street, there is the venerable Mellos Diner. Mellos itself hails from at least 1949 and bears the name of its then registered owner, Gabkop Mellos. The space, however, is older, originating as an ice cream shop. Montreal native Martin Fremeth purchased the diner in 2011, partnering with the late Leisa Louise Bell, a longtime server. During the day, short-order cooks serve a traditional diner menu to regulars who settle into 1970s deuces and four-tops: greasy two-egg breakfasts with bacon and toast, hamburgers and whistle dogs. In the evening, Chef Mike Franks takes over, serving creative ethnic-inspired diner fare like pork dumplings, trini doubles, battered and fried Brussels sprouts, chicken katsu sandwiches and the best patty melt in the city. Franks comes to Mellos by way of Toronto's defunct Barrio Lounge and Ottawa's Kinki's Asian-fusion restaurant.

Outside the ByWard Market, there are now neighbourhoods with high densities of restaurants, eateries and specialty food shops beyond traditional Little Italy and Chinatown: Hintonburg, West Wellington Village, Beechwood, Westboro and Glebe. We have gastro-alleys and epicurean rows.

Consider Hooch at 180 Rideau Street (Ottawa's second bourbon bar, serving modern twists on Kentucky-inspired fare with a nod to New Orleans),

Venerable Mellos Diner, the 1970s-era diner that hails from the 1940s. It's not hipster when it's history.

Town at 296 Elgin Street (smaller plates of modern Italian fare), OZ Kafe at 361 Elgin Street (known for its forays into authentic Korean cuisine, with local ingredients and Chef Appreciation Nights that foster community amongst the restaurant industry), Union Local 613 at 315 Somerset Street West (Ottawa's first bourbon bar and paragon of Canadian-ized southern comfort dining), Back Lane Café at 1087 Wellington Street West (Middle Eastern flavours prepared by the hearth), Wellington Gastropub at 1325 Wellington Street West (beer-inspired gastronomy and now nanobrewery) and Two Six {Ate} at 268 Preston Street (a play on Union, but with Canadian takes on Italian tapas).

There are hotel restaurants in Ottawa that choose not to serve the usual suspect mediocrity that earned them their unfortunate stereotype. Diners will not find plates of chicken fingers and French fries for the kids on the menu. Mostly hosted in independent and boutique hotels, these restaurants display atypical traits in trying to be local destinations: emphasis on quality, freshest products, engaged service and stimulating surroundings. The longstanding ARC Lounge at ARC The Hotel on Slater Street (140) is one such restaurant. Another rite-of-passage kitchen, many of Ottawa's chef entrepreneurs worked the line at the ARC, from René Rodriquez to Steve Mitton. Now under Jason Duffy, the menu showcases regional ingredients prepared with affordable sophistication: pork belly with Brussels sprouts, grilled haloumi with bone marrow, grilled strip loin with spot prawn popcorn and house pancetta and burnt orange Mariposa duck breast with kalamata gnocchi. Duffy's former sous, Stephen Lasalle, operates The Albion Rooms at the Novotel Hotel on Nicholas Street (33). A rustic take on the gastropub set in a business hotel, the Albion Rooms is the result of collaboration between its owner and U.K.'s Gorgeous Group. Having opened in March 2013, Albion Rooms serves modern Canadian takes on English food (Scotch eggs, thrice-cooked chips, kedgeree and Eton mess), with craft cocktails.

Another notable hotel restaurant is Perspectives at the Brookstreet Hotel in Kanata, a west end suburb. Opened by Chef Michael Blackie in 2003 after his return from running the kitchens at the Oberoi in Bali, his new team earned Perspectives four CAA/AAA diamonds within its first four months. Present chef Clifford Lyness continues the tradition with his own style of casual, modern contemporary cuisine: confit pork belly with smoked cheddar pierogi, pan-seared scallops with mushrooms and celeriac puree and Nagano pork chop with Brussels sprouts and house-cured bacon. After a stint as executive chef for the National Arts Centre, Blackie is now operating his own restaurant, NEXT, in Stittsville (6400 Hazeldean Road), serving his

Chef Patrick Garland of Absinthe Café, preparing Crêpe Suzette.

brand of thoughtful ethnic twists on contemporary fare: tom kha gai, salt and pepper squid, rib-eye steak tartare, Blackie's Indian chicken and "Dark and Stormy" pork belly steamed buns.

On Wellington Street West in Hintonburg, there is Absinthe Café. Its chef, Patrick Garland, being an ardent traditionalist when it comes to fine food, has quite the collection of French copper cookware, numbering almost two hundred pieces. His menu is a balance of classical technique, international inspiration and local ingredients. At Absinthe, you will find sauce grebiche, mushroom duxelle, celeriac remoulade and pâté de campagne on the same menu as Korean barbecue quail. A playful roster, some of the more creative charcuterie plates in Ottawa are served here. One featured a duck confit pogo. A restaurant that opened on Holland Avenue in a much smaller space in 2003, three menu items persevere here: the hanger steak frites, escargot gratin and the "Benevolent" burger. The burger, which is made from hanger steak trim, is benevolent because one dollar from each one sold goes to the Cornerstone women's shelter. Garland is an alumnus of Claire de Lune and ambitious former Maplelawn Café, which is now the Ottawa Keg Manor.

With the food truck Relish the Flavour operating on campus, students at the University of Ottawa can enjoy S'Mac N'Cheese at any time.

Street food pioneer Jackie Joliffe of Stone Soup Food Works peeks out of the service window of her truck, Sweet Pea.

Angry Dragonz, part of Ottawa's new food truck scene, offers Asian fusion fare—chicken skewers on the left and cumin lamb skewers on the right.

Patricia Larkin of venerable Black Cat Bistro is one of the city's top chefs. Her career includes a stint as pastry chef at Beckta's.

Brothers Beer Bistro has a "beer first" philosophy. A component of beer is used as an ingredient in every dish. For brunch, there's poached eggs, beer-braised pork belly and spaetzle.

Ottawa is now addicted to artisanal bread thanks to Chef Kevin Mathieson. There are daily lineups at Art-Is-In Bakery to purchase his breads, French pastries and baked goods or dine in the restaurant.

The Benevolent Hanger Steak Burger from Absinthe Café. One dollar from every burger goes to Cornerstone Housing for Women, an emergency women's shelter.

Ottawa's highly decorated Atelier Restaurant only serves a twelve-course blind tasting menu. Chef Marc Lepine is known for his modernist plates.

At El Camino, Chef Matt Carmichael and his crew serve some of the city's best tacos. A menu of Mexican and Asian influences, it's become the darling of the food scene.

In Chinatown, Hung Sum serves dim sum dishes all day, made fresh to order. Here, shrimp har gow is a dim sum staple.

For more than seventy years, Mellos has been serving great diner-style food. However, its "After Dark" menu is a hidden gem. Chef Michael Frank prepares lots of comfort foods.

Murray Street Kitchen's potacco with house pulled pork was featured on Season 2 of *You Gotta Eat Here* on Food Network Canada.

Above: Chef René Rodriguez serves finer dining takes on Mexican cuisine with Roman and Basque (Spanish) influences at Navarra. His skills earned him the title Top Chef Canada (Season 4).

Left: At NEXT, "the Board" features more than fifteen elements, from eggs to pastries, meats, pancakes and sweets. It's a luxurious brunch for two.

The Dutch Baby at Edgar is the talk of the town. A crispy, puffy pancake, but custardy inside, it comes with pork belly, cheddar, chunky apple purée and maple syrup.

Garlic ramps sold at the Ottawa Farmers' Market is a sign that spring has finally arrived in the nation's capital.

Rainbow Swiss chard is sold at many stalls at the Ottawa Farmers' Market. Its large green leaves with orange, yellow, white and red stems makes it a beauty.

From September to early November, a bumper crop of various squashes makes for a colourful display at any farmers' market.

There are more than a dozen pho houses in Chinatown and many more across the city. This spicy beef stewed noodle soup, "bo kho" comes from Pholicious in Chinatown.

Seed to Sausage is best known for its fermented salami, pancetta, guanciale, fresh sausages and an array of deli-style and smoked meats. Everything is made by hand.

Seed to Sausage hosts an annual "Day of the Pig" party featuring top local artisan food producers. It is also a thank-you to its customers.

Ottawa is the shawarma capital of the country. A platter heaping with rice, pickled turnips, potatoes, garlic sauce, salad, hummus and chicken, this is a favourite at Shawarma Palace.

Top: Freshly made Momofuku-style ramen is served for lunch at Sidedoor Contemporary Kitchen and Bar.

Left: Potato soup served with escargot, blood sausage, fried bread and parsley stems at Social Restaurant and Lounge.

Suzy Q, Ottawa's only gourmet doughnut shop, has lineups out the door every week. The maple bacon doughnut is a crowd favourite.

No one can make a Scotch egg quite like Chef Stephen La Salle at The Albion Rooms. This tourtière Scotch egg is served with Québécois "chow chow" (fruit ketchup).

Breakfast pizza from Flat Bread Pizza Company includes smoked pork sausage, duck fat fried potatoes, cheese curds and an egg.

An ice cream sandwich from Pascale's Ice Cream makes a fabulous treat anytime, especially in the summer. Its sinfully rich ice cream has locals hankering for more.

Above: In the fall, Lyle Slater drives his homemade apparatus to harvest cranberries at Upper Canada Cranberries. It is the only commercial cranberry farm in Eastern Ontario.

Left: Continuing the tradition of showcasing Canadian seasonal ingredients, Executive Chef John Morris of the National Arts Centre offers a tempura prawn po-boy for concertgoers.

Above: The "cheese" board at ZenKitchen is a testament to the innovative vegan cuisine by former chef Kyle Mortimer-Proulx.

Left: The Ottawa Tulip Festival celebrates Canada's role in liberating the Dutch during the Second World War and the appreciation of the safe haven given to members of Holland's exiled royal family.

The Anomalies

ZenKitchen on Somerset Street West was an anomaly that many did not think would last past its first year of business. The high-end vegan restaurant was launched in 2009 by a political analyst turned restaurateur and marketing expert turned chef. Then husband and wife, Loan and Chef Caroline Ishii had field-tested their unique concept with what were Ottawa's first pop-up food events before throwing off the shackles of their salaried and cubicled lives. But neither really expected the long hours or the tiny margins that is food service. ZenKitchen's opening was chronicled in a thirteen-episode reality show (*The Restaurant Adventures of Caroline and Dave*) that was aired on the W Network and later picked up by the Asian Food Channel. Ishii would go on to win back-to-back silver medals at the prestigious Gold Medal Plates culinary competition and fundraiser for the Canadian Olympic Foundation in 2010 and 2011. Also in 2011, Ishii and Loan celebrated the restaurant's inclusion in the Lonely Planet's Guide of Canada. Following a death in the family, Ishii left ZenKitchen in 2013, appointing Kyle Mortimer-Proulx chef.

Mortimer-Proulx, an alumnus of Perspectives at the Brookstreet Hotel under Chefs Michael Blackie and Clifford Lyness, led the kitchen for two years. He changed its direction from Japanese-inspired to more Euro-centric farm-to-table fine dining. He even innovated vegan cheeses made from cashews and a quinoa culture. This year, his labours earned him an invitation to compete in Gold Medal Plates. After a brief closure, ZenKitchen reopened in August 2014 with a new chef and pared-down menu. Mortimer-Proulx has gone on to become chef at Lowertown Brewery in the ByWard Market. His former sous, West De Castro, has gone on to open Clover Food and Drink on Bank Street.

In 2007, Chef Marc Lepine worked to modernize the menu at the venerable Courtyard Restaurant, replacing its continental items (jumbo shrimp cocktail, French onion soup, beef Wellington, veal Oscar and chicken Kiev) with more modern small plates, sometimes with molecular twists. In 2008, he opened a restaurant on Rochester Street (540) behind Little Italy, called Atelier, embracing those twists. During the renovations to what was once a Thai restaurant, he staged with Chef Grant Achatz at Alinea Restaurant in Chicago.

Today, diners have seen the rise and fall of molecular food. Almost clichéd plates of spheres in foam no longer excite, but the techniques remain. Stalwart proponents of modernist cuisine apply them to create dishes that celebrate ingredients and convey ideas. One practitioner of what he deems "hyper modern 'new Canadian'" is Marc Lepine. At Atelier, he and his team assemble thoughtful multi-course menus that represent the "now" of food. No à la carte menu, diners dine blind. But plates are constructed to appeal to every kind of diner. They are also feasts for the senses. Imagine creative dishes with ahi tuna, elk, smoked avocado, parsnip and beet. In 2012, Lepine and his team won a gold medal at the Canadian Culinary Championships, representing the National Capital Region after taking gold at Gold Medal Plates the year before. The Canadian Culinary Championships consists of three competitions spread over two days, with eight distinguished judges. Another rite-of-passage kitchen, Lepine's former chef de cuisine, Sarah McGregor, went on to work at Beckta Dining and Wine and Allium Restaurant, spending a short amount of time at The Manx. Pastry Chef Michael Holland went on to open Holland's Cake and Shake, his answer to what a modern malt shop would look like—only Cake and Shake serves Holland's creative pastries.

PARAGON OF SERVICE

One of the restaurateurs responsible for initiating a shift in the restaurant industry is Stephen Beckta. His eponymous flagship on Nepean Street, Play Food and Wine in the ByWard Market on York Street and Gezellig on Richmond Road stand as examples of finer dining and quality service.

Young Beckta grew up on Elgin Street, attending a nearby public school. Already an entrepreneur at an early age, he would use his two-dollar stipend for lunch to purchase chips and pop from a corner store and fries from House of Georgie's. These he would resell at a healthy markup to his classmates. His parents never noticed his profiting from lunch. Mom worked as a server. Dad operated a press mostly for restaurants, printing menus and chits. Oftentimes, he would be paid in trade (such as Chinese food).

"Café Colonnade was [one of] Dad's biggest clients. I used to go to the Metcalfe location after school for a small pizza and root beer,"[15] reminisced Beckta. "You could say the entrepreneurial spirit was family entrenched."

Moving on to high school, he enrolled in Cairine Wilson Secondary School, but while his classmates concentrated on their studies, Beckta worked full time during his evenings and weekends, amassing more than forty hours

Restaurateur Stan Ages's Yesterday's on Sparks Street; Stephen Beckta worked here as a teenager.

per week at mostly casual restaurants along the Elgin strip and within the ByWard Market. Working first as a busboy then server and sometimes cook, he found himself doing the rounds: Malibu Jack's (which would become the Elgin Street Diner), Yesterday's (then owned by Stan Ages), O'Toole's, Peter's Pantry and Dunn's. By the time he arrived at the Ritz 3, George Monsour had moved on. Jimmy Saikely had already converted former Tibidz on Nepean Street to a Ritz 3. Beckta would help open the Ritz 3 on Clarence Street. While working at the Ritz, he was introduced to wine and enrolled at Algonquin College for its sommelier program. Beckta graduated with honours in 1997 and became the Ritz's wine director.

From the Ritz, he would travel to New York City to visit a lady friend he met at a wedding. There, he was introduced to Daniel Boulud, celebrated French chef and restaurateur. Boulud hired him. The management at newly opened Café Boulud may have mistakenly assumed that the "Ritz" on Beckta's résumé was the luxury hotel. As the future award-winning restaurant's new sommelier, Beckta moved on from serving $40 bottles of wine to $8,000 bottles of wine. Suffice it to say, he spent every waking hour that he was not working studying wine. Working an average fifteen hours a day, he fell asleep with books on the subject. His fresh face and amassed knowledge, however, would be noticed by *New York Times* writer Amanda Hester, who did a piece about him in 2000. His was the new face of wine.

After two years at Boulud, Beckta met restaurateur Danny Meyer and worked at Eleven Madison Park, which had just been issued two stars by the *New York Times*. Inspired by Meyer's award-winning commitment to service, he originally asked to work at Grammercy Tavern, but the maitre'd advised him that he "wouldn't learn anything." He needed to find a place that required his help. "With Daniel, we had to be the best! With Danny, we had to be the most caring. " Meyer would go on to publish a book on what he deems "enlightened hospitality," called *Setting the Table*. Accordingly, service and hospitality are separate but intertwined.

At Eleven Madison Park, Beckta studied the New York style of hospitality for two years, learning how to serve guests. By the time he left, Eleven Madison Park had doubled its standing with the *New York Times*. Beckta would later tell Kirstin Endemann of the *Ottawa Citizen* that the principles are simple: "If you take care of the staff, the customers, the suppliers, and the community, then the bottom line will take care of itself."

At just twenty-nine years old, he had worked at two of the top restaurants in Manhattan and had a commitment to travel to Paris, courtesy of Meyer, to

Respected restaurateur and former New York City sommelier Stephen Beckta. *Photo used with permission from Stephen Beckta.*

stage for two weeks under the management of Alain Ducasse. His prestigious sojourn would end after he met Maureen Cunningham at another wedding, this time at the Museum of Nature in Ottawa. Smitten, he proposed to Cunningham on the Brooklyn Bridge on their way to Dan Barber's Blue Hill restaurant in Greenwich Village on New Year's Eve.

Returning to Ottawa, he opened Beckta Dining and Wine in May 2003 at the location of the Ritz restaurant that propelled him to New York City. "George Monsour helped me write the business plan for Beckta. He was on the original board." He added, "My first one, restaurateur-ing, was a roller-coaster ride."

Executive Chef Michael Moffatt at the end of service at Play Food and Wine in the ByWard Market.

Hiring Steve Vardy, then freshly released from Café Henry Burger and after a stint at Kinki's, the menu at Dining and Wine consisted of good but unpretentious food with some multicultural twists. Beckta wanted to make fine dining approachable and accessible, so he offered tasting menus, canapés and signature personal service. Glowing accolades followed from Ottawa's restaurant critic Anne DesBrisay and then Air Canada's *En Route* magazine, which chose Dining and Wine as one of the best new restaurants in Canada. The dining room was soon booked weeks in advance. The restaurant earned consecutive four CAA/AAA diamonds thereafter. "We would have five diamonds, but we had too many banquettes and no parking."

Michael Moffatt, who studied at culinary school with Steve Vardy, joined Beckta as sous three to four months after the restaurant opened. They staged together at River Café in New York City. In 2006, Vardy left to work at Joshua Bishop's Whalesbone Oysterhouse on Bank Street after its inaugural year. He would take new recruit Steve Wall with him. Moffatt became chef and partner thereafter. Incidentally, Steve Wall would go on to open award-winning Supply and Demand (1335 Wellington Street West) in the West Wellington Village in 2013.

After a disappointing meal in the ByWard Market, Beckta and his wife walked by a building with a "For Rent" sign, offering basement and ground and second floors. Number 1 York Street had been a "Euro café" back in the day. It was most recently a failed high-end kitchenware store with a large window display. Play Food and Wine would open in the location in January 2009. The combination of small plates and wine bar was another hit with Ottawa diners.

Three years later, in October 2012, Beckta opened Gezellig on Richmond Road in the Westboro neighbourhood. Gezellig was a bit of a setback for Beckta, as he had misjudged the neighbourhood. Originally, he had thought that a family-style atmosphere with an accessible menu would work well. But just as he had had to adjust his initial designs to accommodate the existing twenty-five-foot windows of the former Toronto Dominion Bank, he also had to adjust his approach to the restaurant. "Gezellig had to develop its own soul. Diners wanted something more in the modern space." Now that Dining and Wine has reached the end of its lease, Beckta has plans to reestablish his flagship restaurant at the Grant House on Elgin Street.

Decades have passed since roast beef houses like Ken Dolan's former Friday's on Elgin fell from grace. Going out for a traditional plate of English-cut roast beef, baked potato, Yorkshire pudding and carrots was all the rage in 1972 when Dolan decided to open a restaurant and piano bar in a heritage building dating back to 1875. His leasing the building, formerly home to parliamentary physician Sir James Alexander Grant, saved it from demolition. Toward the end of Friday's thirty-year tenure, increasing rent, decreasing patronage and pressure from developers forced Dolan to close its doors. However, large chain steakhouses continue the tradition of prime rib and tenderloin tournedos with value-added but forgettable sides like lobster tail, garlic shrimp and soup and iceberg salad.

For his new Dining and Wine establishment, Beckta promises to give people a chance to exhale, take a respite and feel cared for again. The new Beckta Dining and Wine will again leverage New York City inspirations, particularly how restaurants like Grammercy Tavern and Blue Hill continue to reinvent themselves to stay relevant.

Burgers Again

One of our current food scene's success stories involves novelty burgers, a restaurant concept called "The Works" and a man named Ion Aimers.

The generation that flocked to Daphne and Victor's for gourmet burgers in the 1970s and 1980s grew up and learned to eat sensibly. But there is still something compelling about a good burger that anyone, young or old, can connect with: a juicy, well-seared patty; drippy melted cheese; and a soft bun. Now imagine having every possible condiment and topping available to customize your burger.

In the finer food world, Aimers is known to partner with talented local chefs to open independent restaurants like the celebrated Fraser Café (7 Springfield Road) and its Table 40 communal dining room. The open kitchen of the six-year-old café is run by award-winning sibling chefs Ross and Simon Fraser. While the menu served at Fraser's is a little more sophisticated, they no doubt hope that you will find their plates equally as compelling.

In 2013, Aimers renovated a cherished diner on the corner of Bank and Arlington Streets, opening Wilf and Ada's Scratch Kitchen. His intention with the refreshed interior and new menu is to continue the legacy left by retired owners Ada Laham and her husband, Wilf. The menu serves soul-satisfying diner fare, though gussied up a bit. For this venture, Aimers partnered with Jessie Duffy and Dominic Paul, both formerly of Fraser Café.

Recently, Aimers opened Segue in a space left behind by a former Valente brothers' Fratelli's at the corner of Bank Street and First Avenue. There he renovated a family-style Italian restaurant, transforming it into an upscale neighbourhood eatery. For this venture, he partnered with former Beckta

Dining and Wine sous Rich Wilson and former Fraser Café server Lindsay Gordon to serve bistro-inspired small plates.

In the business world, Aimers is known for parlaying his "gourmet" burger concept into a sale to Oakville-based Fresh Brands Inc., which has taken the local chain he created to serve almost sixty-one types of burgers nationally, opening twenty more restaurants to date.

The first Works opened in December 2001 in a tiny 750-square-foot space in trendy New Edinburgh. A total of six more locations would appear over the next nine years, from the Glebe to Kanata in the west end and Orleans in the east end.

Ottawans flocked to the locations, with their industrial-themed décor, lining up out the door when the tables filled. Disarming, each seemed a cross between a playground and boiler room, with tin sheeting, exposed brick, copper pipes, valves that you want to move, pressure gauges you want to read, handles you want to turn and false metal door covers that don't open. Fittingly, food is served on lined baking trays. Drinks are served in Pyrex measuring cups.

Somehow, Aimers knew that diners had grown tired of fast-food burgers, each one identical to the next. It takes a special kind of genius to determine the right time in the ever-changing marketplace to slather Kraft Dinner on a burger, give it a fanciful name (the "San Francisco Treat") and sell it for ten dollars.

A serial restaurateur, the Montreal-born Aimers's résumé includes a first break at The Keg. He also managed a Montana's Cookhouse Saloon and LA Wings in the ByWard Market. The concept for the Works actually came to him during one of his shifts at The Keg.

Almost two decades later, with an upswing in the economy, he gambled that he could reintroduce the burger experience—handmade patties made from never-frozen meat, grilled to order and topped however you saw fit.

With three Zazaza locations, Aimers looks to be trying to do same thing with pizza. This time, instead of a factory's boiler room, he seems to be setting the scene for his twenty-six novelty pizzas in a faux-glitzy theatre, complete with stage lights, red curtain frames and giant ornate mirrors. And yes, the "Scary Roommate" pizza on the menu is slathered in Kraft Dinner and hot dogs.

The Darling

The "darling restaurant" of today is El Camino (380 Elgin Street). What Ion Aimers did for the lowly burger and is attempting for pizza, Matt Carmichael has done for the taco at his wildly popular El Camino taqueria and bar—only Carmichael's concept is chef-driven and part of a back-to-basics trend for finer food.

Carmichael is an award-winning chef who has worked with some recognized names in Ottawa and Toronto, including Chefs John Taylor, Susur Lee (then of Susur), David Lee (then of Splendido), Kei Ng of KEI and Michael Blackie (then of Perspectives). In 2009, Carmichael won a bronze medal at the Canadian Culinary Championships, representing the National Capital Region after taking gold at Gold Medal Plates the year before.

At El Camino, like his short-lived pop-up dinners at Mellos Diner, Carmichael concentrates on the food. Service is well coordinated and thoughtful. Drinks are creative. But there is no emphasis on décor. Stark and austere, there are few wall accents. There is a pinball machine in the corner, a favourite from Carmichael's childhood.

El Camino's kitchen serves plates of Carmichael's take on Southeast Asian "hawker fare" (crispy prawn betel leaf, salt and pepper squid and scallop crudo with house-made xo sauce) and tacos (braised and seared ox tongue, crispy fried fish, lamb, pork and beef). The flour tortillas are reminiscent of Lone Star's. Both are freshly made throughout service. Both are soft and yielding. And both grill up nicely, holding up well to wet taco fodder.

Most days, the lineup climbs the stairs from the sub-street-level eatery on Elgin at 5:00 p.m. At 5:30 p.m., the doors open, and the restaurant gets "slammed." Every seat fills. Servers race to distribute one-page menus and list off the daily special that often runs out an hour later. Niall Robertson-Patterson, the gentle general of the bar, looks on with two other bartenders as craft cocktail orders come in. Get the first turnover served: drinks first, food shortly thereafter.

The place stays elbow-to-elbow slammed until 2:00 a.m., last call. The atmosphere truly is electric as rush after rush comes and goes. Just about everyone in the opening lineup finds seats in the atypical dining room with a meandering bar, a few high-tops (deuces and four-tops), a communal picnic-style table and pair of booths for large groups. Then the host starts the unenviable task of creating the wait list of cellphone numbers to text when

The service window at El Camino is busy regardless of snow, rain, heat or gloom of night.

seats free up. Above him is a sign that reads, "Don't be a dick." First come and first seated, El Camino does not accept reservations.

The impossible taqueria averages an unheard-of six hundred covers any given Tuesday. It averages eight hundred covers most Sundays and retails three hundred tacos from its public-facing takeaway window daily. That window is cash only. Don't think that the window is any less busy in the winter. Former cooks estimated serving between 100 and 150 people per day this past winter, even when temperatures fell to minus 30 degrees Celsius.

Culinary School

Two culinary schools help to power Ottawa's restaurant industry, training today's cooks who may become tomorrow's chefs.

In North America, the name "Cordon Bleu" stands for fine French cuisine. Historically, the name originated in 1578, when King Henry III of France established L'Ordre des Chevaliers du Saint-Esprit (Order of the

Holy Spirit). Knights of this order wore a golden cross attached by a blue sash or ribbon, which became known as "cordon bleus."

French journalist Marthe Distel established the Cordon Bleu school in Paris in 1895, and it became synonymous with high skill in the culinary arts. Andre Contreau, whose family is linked to French Contreau liqueur and Remy Martin cognac, acquired the school, which was known to have produced a century of quality chefs, in 1984. In 1988, he bought an eight-year-old French cooking school in Ottawa that was located on the fourth floor of a Prince of Wales Drive high-rise building, establishing the first Cordon Bleu Culinary Arts institute outside France. Keeping founder Eleanor Orser on to operate the school, tuition to earn La Grand Diplome cost $40,000. During its first year, Orser accepted no more than twenty-four students for the day courses and twelve for the evening courses to complete Level 1 of the three-part "classic cycle" of instructions. Orser earned her Grand Diplome from Le Cordon Bleu in 1979. Unique to North America, Le Cordon Bleu Ottawa would outgrow its space.

Marking the beginning of the end of exclusive fine dining in the National Capital Region, Le Cercle Universitaire D'Ottawa (453 Laurier Avenue), a former private club in the Sandy Hill neighbourhood, closed its doors in August 2000, selling its then 123-year-old stately mansion, former home to a lumber baron, to pay its creditors. Founded in 1958 to cater to Ottawa's French elite, Le Cercle required members to pay a $1,500 initiation fee and annual dues to partake of the fine French cuisine served in its luxurious dining rooms. Male members were required to wear a jacket and tie. Business documents were accordingly not permitted. As years passed, Le Cercle found that it could not compete with the rise of new restaurants in Ottawa and Hull. Notable kitchen alumni include George Laurier and Tracey Black, who would go on to own and operate Epicuria Fine Foods and Catering. Le Cordon Bleu bought the property for $1.4 million and converted it into a cooking school and restaurant.

Offering a reorganized Grand Diplome program in 2000, the new cooking school prided itself on rigid hands-on training, teaching technical skills. Its program was practical, including no classes in kitchen administration or management. To serve as a mentor, celebrated chef Frédéric Filliodeau opened the first in North America Le Cordon Bleu restaurant, Signatures, in February 2001. He came by way of Montreal Casino's Nuances restaurant, which had just earned five CAA/AAA diamonds. Before that, he was deputy to French master chef Georges Blanc at his eponymous restaurant in France that earned three Michelin stars. More of a demonstration restaurant, students did not cook for diners but rather observed highly trained chefs practice strict French technique with Canadian ingredients. In 2004, Filliodeau-lead Signatures earned four CAA/AAA diamonds. Two years later, the restaurant earned five. That fall, Chef Yannick Anton would replace Filliodeau as executive chef, and celebrated pastry chef Christian Faure would join him. The new brigade continued the tradition of an elaborate and luxurious menu until 2008, when a change in direction to reflect the new realities of French cuisine closed Signatures but soon opened Le Cordon Bleu Bistro. Briefly a student-operated bistro, Anton and his sous would take the reins thereafter. Filliodeau is now executive chef at the Sheraton Ottawa Hotel on Albert Street (150), responsible for its in-house Carleton Grill.

The Algonquin College School of Hospitality and Tourism has a markedly different approach, actively partnering with the local restaurant industry to teach and apprentice prospective cooks and chefs. Students enroll in programs of classes taught by resident and part-time chef instructors to gain skills and earn credentials. A common goal is the Red Seal, a national trade designation that consists of passing a standardized interprovincial exam and completing about six thousand hours of field work. Algonquin offers nine hundred hours through its hands-on classes and in-house student-operated 130-seat restaurant, Le Restaurant.

Chef Kyle Mortimer-Proulx explained, "We get many strong candidates from Algonquin College. It is turning out very well-qualified graduates who benefit from partnerships with industry."[16]

Culinary-related certificates and diplomas have become popular, causing increased enrollment. In 1971, the first program, designed by founder (and late chef) Tony Casagrande, attracted only 49 students. Forty years later, there were 450 students working their way through the culinary arts and management, hospitality, nutrition and sommelier programs. It is no longer unusual for students to enroll and complete training at both Le Cordon Bleu Ottawa Culinary Arts Institute and Algonquin College. Besides practical skills, like learning how to make classical stocks and sauces, programs also teach menu planning and food and beverage management, business aspects behind operating a kitchen and restaurant.

In 2011, to address increased demand and the increasingly sophisticated student, Algonquin launched a four-year-degree hospitality program. This program was designed with guidance from the restaurant industry, including alumni and past instructors, to help students develop foundational basics, practical experience through frontline exposure (two five-hundred-hour work terms) and business and management skills. The degree is intended to enable graduates to compete for higher positions in the field.

A Complicated Crisis

According to Rebecca L. Spang's *The Invention of the Restaurant*, restaurants owe their existence to pre-revolutionary French statesman, entrepreneur and banker Mathurin Roze de Chantoiseau. He first proposed an establishment that served restorative broths called "restaurants" in 1769. Ironically, the concept was but a small component of a treatise on fiscal reform. Roze de Chantoiseau's scheme to replace national debt with "Letters of Credit" of real value was recognized by the court of King Louis XVI in 1789.

So, restaurants as we know them did not emerge from the efforts or imaginations of a bustling kitchen. Until Roze de Chantoiseau, they were medicinal remedies prepared to restore lost strength or cure "weakness of chest." Often prescribed by physicians, restaurants could be wine or brandy to lift spirits or condensed bouillons made from meat and vegetables for nourishment.

Spang explained that food was prepared in the Parisian home. Farmers were purveyors of produce. Butchers, charcutiers and rotisseurs were purveyors of meat, be it raw, prepared as sausages and cured meats or "cooked" (either larded or roasted). Travelers depended on innkeepers. Cook-caterers prepared complete meals mostly for the aristocracy. Food in the French capital was largely functional, far from notable.

It was not until the nineteenth century that restaurants became spaces for pleasurable freedoms, complete with printed menus showcasing a culinary repertoire. Restaurants changed from being public/private spaces for political discussion to institutions for cultural expression. They created a new market for hospitality and taste.

The reality of the modern restaurant is a little more complicated, which explains why, despite the explosion of restaurants in Ottawa, diners still feel they have few choices. On the diner side, consider recent media coverage of dining room unrest. Chefs actively condemn murky, dark or strangely filtered smartphone snapshots of their plates. Restaurateurs blame callous patrons with smartphones for slowing down service. Some threaten to ban photography altogether. Restaurateurs publicly shame unruly patrons on social media: no shows with reservations, anyone who lingers after food and beverage have been cleared from tables and drunkards up to their usual antics.

On the restaurant's side, consider this: you work on a brigade in a professional kitchen at a restaurant. Your day likely starts early in the morning, prepping and making sure that critical dish components are ready for service, be it lunch or dinner. How much prep is done is based on expected turnover. The dining room will fill and empty repeatedly.

Tables will seat patrons who are more sensitized to food than ever. Everyone is armed with a smartphone, everyone is quick to critique and everyone has preconceived ideas about what is good service and what is good food. Restaurant criticism has changed. Diners have shifted away from trusted professional sources to wading through comments to determine consensus. They crowd-source opinions expressed in people's brief retellings of their dining at a restaurant. Newspapers hire freelancers or task another existing resource with the role of restaurant reviewer. Anonymity is no longer required. Visiting a restaurant multiple times to account for an anomaly becomes prohibitively expensive.

Some diners are better traveled than others, carrying diversified collections of food experiences. Unfortunately, value tends to be determined by how a dish compares with something someone has seen on the Food Network, often with a smug Gordon Ramsay bleeping obscenities in the background. Alternatively, a case of traveler's arrogance will cause the diner to question the authenticity of a dish—"I've had better in France." With most people addicted to social media, diners expect immediate satisfaction.

Working professional kitchens are a combination of assembly line and choreographed ballet. Unnecessary movement is minimized to ensure that dishes are put together efficiently and accurately. Everyone has specific roles in a rigid hierarchy, with each role dependent on the next. Physical space is at a premium. Waste is taboo. Precision is celebrated. Mistakes can make the difference between a satisfied customer and an irate one who takes his or her concerns about food or service to Yelp without resolving the issues with the restaurant. Many revenge reviews read like cathartic outbursts keyed angrily on the way out the door.

What happens when an unexpected forty-five people show up on a usually slow night, it being the beginning of spring break? You make do.

Small independent restaurants operate with razor-thin margins, so rising food costs, changes in regulations and increases in minimum wage, property tax or permit fees could force increase prices or cuts to staff. Many restaurateurs and chefs close their businesses when the uncertainty of a full dining room becomes too high. Everything reflects an ugly truth. It is becoming increasingly difficult to make a living. When your wallet is near empty, you are less likely to consider other people. Time is money, and you haven't any to spare.

Forget common sense etiquette.

Perhaps a little hospitality from both sides of the table is due.

Chapter 5

GUZZLING THE SUDS

> *Bytown, as Ottawa was first called, owed its early importance to lumbering and as the terminus of the Rideau Canal, an important military work… instead it became a wild and turbulent village, full of lumbermen, Irishmen and liquor.*
>
> *–Edwin Guillet, historian*

Beer is perhaps the world's greatest and most historically significant beverage. Every batch that has ever been brewed, every pint poured, shared and consumed, has a story to tell. The flavours and ingredients used reflect the region and the people behind it. Ottawa is no exception. The national capital region has its own stories.

From the days before Ottawa existed, when it was little more than a rough-and-tumble town called Bytown, this city has always had a love affair with locally brewed beer. With the recent emergence of craft breweries, Ottawans today may think that their city's ability to brew its own beer is in keeping with the trends. Today, little physical evidence remains of previous breweries and distilleries as buildings were demolished as Ottawa modernized throughout the twentieth century. Entrepreneurs brewed beer and distilled spirits long before Canada became a country in 1867 and even before Bytown was renamed Ottawa in 1855. Former food reviewer Kathleen Walker eloquently wrote in her book *Ottawa's Repast*, "In a way, the history of beer and hard liquor is the history of the Ottawa Valley itself."

There are twenty-three lock stations located along the waterway from Kingston to Ottawa. Here, Locks 1–8 form the largest single set of locks on the entire Rideau system.

The Rideau Canal is the oldest continuously operated canal system in North America. It played a pivotal role in the early development of Ottawa.

By mid-nineteenth century, Bytown was growing rapidly due to the arrival of English, Irish and French settlers and the British army. As the population and local industries grew, so did the distilleries, breweries and taverns. Not only was beer considered an everyday beverage, but it was also deemed a "healthy" drink. Bytown was behind the times when it came to modern luxuries such as tap water. Residents had to wait until the mid-1870s, when construction of underground pipes and sewers began, for households to have running water. Fresh local water supplies were extremely polluted due to human and animal waste, sewage, refuse and logs from nearby mills. With precious pure water available, beer was rather an important element of the pioneer's diet. Beer is boiled during the brewing process, thus making it safer to drink.

As early settlers depended on beer, it was vital that they made their own with available resources. They either grew their own or went foraging for hops, fruits, barley, herbs and green spring roots of spruce trees. The presence of the British military served to only fuel Bytown's thirst for beer. As Ian Bowering described in his book *The Art and Mystery of Brewing in Ontario*, beer was part of the daily rations of the soldiers. In fact, military men expected and received ale, with four to six pints a day considered the norm. As the number of settlers of British descent increased, their beer attitudes and brewing knowledge had a significant influence on our beer culture, especially on the beer styles.

The construction of the Rideau Canal also had a crucial impact on the growth of Bytown. Starting in the summer of 1826, the building of the canal saw the arrival of thousands of labourers and tradesmen such as stonemasons, contractors, engineers, blacksmiths, carpenters and teamsters, working along the two-hundred-kilometre route of the canal at various locations. Cutting trees, installing locks, building lock houses and military fortifications, draining swamps, drilling and hauling rocks were just some of the tasks required. Adding in the large influx of Scottish and Irish workers and the establishment of the community of Bytown, this was the economic beginnings of Ottawa. Similarly, as construction of the canal intensified, so, too, did the demand for services like shelter and accommodation—and, of course, alcohol.

When the canal opened in 1832, the population of Bytown was 1,500. Within twenty years, it had increased to 7,760.

SOME OF OTTAWA'S EARLIEST BREWS

Due to inconsistent recordkeeping in the 1800s, it is difficult to distinguish who opened the first brewery or distillery. Whereas a brewery is a dedicated building for the making of beer, a distillery is simply a place where liquor is manufactured. According to Bowering, the Victoria Brewery (1829–99) was a pioneer brewery at the corner of Rochester and Wellington Streets in Rochesterville, which is the present-day neighbourhood of Centretown West. Constructed by John Rochester, the brewery and sometimes distillery produced two popular beers: the double stout and its India pale ale. However, as Rochesterville was not annexed by the City of Ottawa until 1888, technically, Victoria Brewery was not located in Bytown.

New Edinburgh, one of the older and more affluent neighbourhoods of modern-day Ottawa, was previously a village, a distinctly separate urban area east of Lower Bytown. Thomas McKay, a Scottish stonemason, was one of many who worked as a contractor on the construction of the Rideau Canal. After acquiring land at the mouth of the Rideau River, he built various mills, a distillery and Rideau Hall, the large stone residence for himself. Built in 1838, Rideau Hall today is the home of the governor general of Canada (1 Sussex Drive). McKay's distillery sold whiskey, which also helped to pay for his large home.

Around the same time, his neighbour Isaac MacTaggart operated a brewery and distillery on the grounds of the present-day French Embassy (42 Sussex Drive) in the 1830s. But as New Edinburgh was not made a part of Ottawa until 1887, MacTaggart also cannot claim to have this city's first brewery.

The first documented brewery belongs to G.R. Burke, a clerk of the Division Court. His brewery was located near the Rideau Canal and operated from as early as 1844 until 1857, when Bowering noted that it disappeared from the files.

From the 1850s to mid-1860s, a number of breweries were recorded in Ottawa (Bytown no longer being its name), including the Chaudière Brewery (1858) by Parris and Smith and George Sterling's brewery at the foot of Rideau Locks. Another brewery (1864), operated by John Doyle, was on Sussex Drive, opposite York Street. There was, however, one brewery that was established during those years that survived well into the twentieth century: Brading's, then known as Union Brewery.

As Allen Winn Sneath described in his book *Brewed in Canada*, Harry Fisher Brading had settled in the Ottawa Valley in 1865 when talks of Confederation was the main topic in Ottawa. Conditions were ideal for Brading to open a brewery, with a continuously growing population and thirsty lumbermen. "It provided the opportunity of a lifeline for the 33-year-old English brewer from the town of Brading on the Isle of Wight," Sneath wrote. With fellow brewers Henry Israel and John Atwood, Brading established Union Brewery along the Ottawa River. Records indicate an address of 461 Wellington Street and Sparks. By 1880, Brading had bought out his partners, becoming the sole owner and changing the brewery's name to Brading's Brewery; he officially renamed it as Brading Brewing Company Limited in 1906. Brading himself had no real competitor until Henry Kuntz established Capital Brewery nearby.

Brading's brands were quite popular with folks along the Ottawa River, going as far west as Kingston, including Brown Stout, Hope Ale Plus 9%, Old Stock Ale and Stag's Head Lager Plus 9%. In April 1900, Ottawa was devastated by a great fire; thousands of homes were left in ashes, with vast stretches of the city in ruins. Brading's buildings, surrounded by lumberyards, were in danger of being destroyed. Together with Harry, loyal lumberjacks formed a bucket brigade around the building, using water handed up from the Ottawa River to save it from certain destruction. Let it be said that Ottawans loved their beer.

Over the years, the brewery went through numerous changes, moving from one location to another. Bottling works were added in 1903, the same year as Harry Brading's passing. Operations were handed over to Brading's son and to a friend, Charles Magee, who later bought out the young Brading's share. Eventually, the business was passed on to Magee's grandson, Edward Plunkett Taylor, who turned it into the cornerstone of a business empire. Buying dozens of other small Ontario breweries, Taylor consolidated and modernized some while closing others. Along with Brading's Brewery, the breweries were amassed and became Canadian Breweries Ltd., later known as Carling O'Keefe in 1969.

OTTAWA BREWERIES AT THE END OF THE TWENTIETH CENTURY

Capital Brewery, once a rival of Brading's, was taken over by Canadian Breweries in 1944. The business became Brading's-Capital Brewery Limited in 1947 and then Brading Breweries Limited (Jubilee Brewery, 1955) after it was expanded and updated as part of Canadian Breweries modernization program. In 1956, the brewery became O'Keefe Brewery but was closed by 1969, when production moved to Toronto. Brading's Brewery would not come to the attention of the public again until early July 2014, when crews working on replacing old sewers along Albert Street unearthed Ottawa's fabled beer tunnel near Lebreton Flats. Hidden from the public, this mysterious tunnel had once been in operation for many years, with men moving endless cases of Brading's and Capital ale, port and lager from the plant to the warehouse, where they were then shipped out on trucks. Leo Deriger, who worked at Brading's in the 1950s and 1960s, has fond memories. "Oh my god, let me tell you. It was the best job you could have. The company treated you good," he said in an interview with *Ottawa Citizen*.

In the 1970s and into the 1980s, Carling O'Keefe was part of the Big Three, along with Molson and Labatt, which dominated the national beer scene. Unfortunately, the status as a national brand was short-lived, as Carling O'Keefe was bought by Elders IXL of Australia in 1987 and then merged with Molson to form Molson Breweries Canada in 1989. However, its beers—the Carling Premier, Red Cap Ale and Old Vienna—continue to be available for purchase.

By the 1990s, scant physical evidence of Ottawa's brewing history remained. While other parts of Ontario had a more vibrant craft beer and brewpub scene, the nation's capital was having difficulty maintaining its new entrants. The microbrewery Ottawa Valley Brewing Company, located in Carleton Place, started in 1985 and was completed the following year. But due to the lengthy licensing process, there were no sales of beer in kegs to licensed establishments until September 1986. With the addition of a bottling machine, though, the brewery had begun selling its product in two- and one-litre bottles to the public by June 1987. Its two mainstay brews were the Ottawa Valley Ale and Bytown Lager. Sadly, within five years, Ottawa Valley Brewing had shut down its operations and voluntarily declared bankruptcy in September 1990. Taxes and low bottle returns were blamed despite steady growth.

When Hart Breweries, also located in Carleton Place, opened in 1991, it became the only brewery east of Toronto. Founder Lorne Hart was confident of competing with the "big boys," Molson and Labatt. Microbreweries across Canada were booming because they offered something the big breweries could not or did not want to make: a distinctive taste. Banking on the difference in taste and the perception of quality to help sell his products, Hart was hopeful. With its award-winning Hart Amber Ale, Festive Brown Ale, Dragons Breath's Ale and Pumpkin Ale, Hart beers were popular all over Eastern Ontario and were even marketed in the United States. But with slow growth, large debts and weak financing, the region's only microbrewery began struggling, reducing staff and seeking protection from creditors. Despite Montreal's Upland Global Corporation becoming a majority shareholder in 1998, the brewery continued to struggle, finally declaring bankruptcy in the fall of 2001. Hart Breweries did come back into business when wealthy investor Peter Harrison from Grenada and his two daughters bought the assets of the brewery in April 2002. Renaming it Banks Canada, Home of Hart Brewers, the North American representatives for Banks Beer decided to brew only Hart's Amber Ale. Banks Beer, considered to be the "beer of Barbados," is highly sought after by Canadians of Caribbean heritage. Although Banks Beer products are available at Liquor Control Board of Ontario (LCBO) stores, the brewery itself no longer operates in Carleton Place.

With no more microbreweries, Ottawa's beer scene looked bleak. It would be some years before the region's hankering for a good craft beer would bring any change.

Guzzling the Suds in 2000s: A New Era

The Clocktower opened its first location on Bank Street between downtown and the Glebe in 1996. Claiming to be the city's original locally run brewpub, Clocktower serves craft beers, with the Kðlsh being its flagship brand. With a total of five house beers—including Clocktower Red, Bytown Brown, Wishart's ESB and a Raspberry Wheat and several seasonal beers—Ottawans could enjoy craft beers with their pub food. However, it was not until the 2006 opening of another brewery about one hundred kilometres east of downtown Ottawa that the city had a renewed interest in local beer.

Beau's All Natural Brewing Company

Launched on July 1, 2006, Beau's, as it is simply known, is the region's most successful microbrewery in recent years. Beau's is headquartered in Vankleek Hill, while the majority of its customers are in Ottawa. Started by the father-and-son team of Tim and Steve Beauchesne, they managed to sell its entire first batch of three thousand litres to nine Ottawa-area bars and restaurants before the official opening date. Within two years, Beau's award-winning Lug Tread lagered ale was available at local LCBO stores and at more than ninety establishments in the Ottawa area.

By July 2009, Beau's Lug Tread was on tap at more than two hundred establishments in Eastern Ontario and selling in nearly every LCBO in the region. By the end of the year, Beau's was supplying a number of bars and LCBOs in the Greater Toronto Area.

Each fall, the Beauchesne family throws a huge party known as Oktoberfest for their staff, the people of Vankleek Hill and for all beer lovers, providing buses for people from Ottawa, Cornwall and Montreal wishing to join in on the festivities. A two-day event, attendees can sample

Some of Beau's best-selling seasonal beers and one-of-a-kind brews have locals lining up at beer markets.

The annual Oktoberfest celebration held by Beau's All Natural Brewing Company in Vankleek Hill draws hundreds of beer enthusiasts from Ottawa, Cornwall and Montreal.

more than a dozen Beau's beers with Bavarian-inspired cuisine by local restaurants. The festival is also an opportunity for the family to give back to the community by supporting several local charities.

Named as one of the province's best microbreweries, Beau's produces several award-winning beers, including seasonal ones. In January 2014, the brewery announced that it would be distributing its brews to retailers across New York State. The opportunity to serve their American consumers has the Beauchesnes excited. Steve admits that they have their hearts set on keeping the beer within a day's drive of the brewery, thereby establishing relationships with the people who serve, sell and drink Beau's beers. Any potential sales in New York State means more exposure but would still allow Beau's to be a local brewery.

THE BIRTH OF NEW CRAFT BREWERIES

The success of Beau's has served as an inspiration for many local entrepreneurs eager to brew their own craft beers. The Beauchesne family actively helps other craft breweries get their start, often offering advice and lending equipment. In 2010, two microbreweries had their launch within weeks of each other with HogsBack Brewing Company opening right before Kichesippi Beer Company. HogsBack currently contracts its brew from a number of craft brewers as the company continues to scout for a permanent location in the city. Meanwhile, Kichesippi's brewery is just west of the downtown core. The names of both breweries have local ties—Hog's Back is the name of a waterfall and a park, and the Ottawa River was originally known as Kichesippi.

Asked why he created Kichesippi, founder Paul Meek explained, "On our travels, Kelly [his wife] and I noticed that when you're in Europe, you visit a little town and it has its own beer. You go to the next town, and it's not available."[17] Meek continues, "We wanted to create something that Ottawa could have as its own experience. So that when people come to Ottawa, they want to try it. We're not going to sell it outside of the national capital region. When people visit Ottawa and ask what they have to try, I want locals to say, 'You can't leave Ottawa without trying a Kichesippi.' We're trying to be something that Ottawa can be proud of."

With three beers available year-round—Natural Blonde, Kichesippi 1855 and Heller Highwater—and five seasonal beers, Kichesippi is well on its way to creating brews in which locals can take pride. Available in 150 retailers and from 180 taps, Ottawans and visitors can all be part of the local experience.

Paul Meek, founder of Kichesippi Beer Company, is dedicated to brewing beers exclusive to the nation's capital.

Inside Kichesippi Beer Company, located at 866 Campbell Avenue. While the machines are whirling away, Spiderman is seen relaxing by a tank.

Three generations of the Deraiche family. On the right is Chris Deraiche, chef/owner of Wellington Gastropub.

Paul admits that while the city is behind on the craft brewery scene compared to other Canadian cities, it is an exciting time, as Ottawa is reestablishing its roots. Since 2010, more microbreweries have opened, generating excitement among beer drinkers. Broadhead Brewing opened in 2011, along with Beyond the Pale in 2012 in Hintonburg and Turtle Island Brewing Company and Covered Bridge Brewing in Kanata and Stittsville. Elsewhere in the Ottawa Valley, Whitewater Brewing in Foresters Falls opened in 2011 and Cassel Brewery a year later in Casselman.

For those looking to tour multiple breweries and have samples but do not want to drive, there is the Brew Donkey. A licensed craft beer–focused liquor delivery service, Brew Donkey strives to deliver all the craft beer the region has to offer. The business also aims to educate people about the options available in the area and the brewing process. Brewery tours are offered, highlighting the beer scene with "brewing, brewpubs and beer bars."

Brewpubs have also established themselves in the region, joining Clocktower in serving pub food with house-made craft beer. Toronto chain Mill Street Brewpub expanded to the capital in January 2012 at Lebreton Flats, within walking distance of downtown Ottawa, and downtown Gatineau. There is also Ashton Brewing Company in Carleton Place, and on the other side of the river, Ottawans can easily get to Brasseurs du Temps and Microbrasserie Gainsbourg. Les 3 Brasseurs has two locations in the city, and there is also Big Rig Brewing Company and Lowertown Brewing Company, the latest addition to the brewpub scene.

Recognized as one of the best restaurants in Ottawa, the Wellington Gastropub is a beer-inspired gastropub and nanobrewery. It brews beer in one-hundred-litre batches that are featured on tap alongside other Ontario craft beers.

The remainder of 2014 appears to be bright, as Toronto-chain brewpub Biermarkt looks set to join the Ottawa market. Dominion City Brewing Company opened the doors of its bottle shop to the public in August. Two new breweries are hoping to open by the end of the year: Waller Street Brewing in downtown off Rideau Street and Whiprsnapr Brewing Company in the west end suburb Bells Corners.

Heading into the future, Ottawa has the opportunity to establish itself as a new beer destination, as we reclaim our heritage and continue to make our mark as a city fully capable of brewing great beer. Asked what they hope to see in the coming years, founders Shane Clark and Rob McIsaac of Beyond the Pale are looking forward to seeing more breweries joining an already crowded market. Whether the scene is sustainable remains to be seen. But with more players, they reason, it will help further elevate the quality of beers and establish more competition. Would it be possible to run out of ideas for new flavours? They laugh and say, "There are all these options that are so flavourful. Beer has so many flavour profiles."[18] Experimenting with various ingredients and thinking of food pairings for each beer is endless.

Chapter 6

FOOD GOES MOBILE

Despite continued efforts to increase the vibrancy and vitality of what seems a missing aspect of the food culture on our shores, North American street food differs substantially from street food overseas, especially in Southeast Asia. They have hawker stalls with bare-bones gear, sometimes consumer appliances and limited fuel. We have professional mobile food service equipment, including generators and refrigeration on board food trucks or carts. They have centuries-old open-air markets that sell as much prepared foods and drinks as they do fresh produce, meats, herbs and spices. We have farmers' markets, food courts and food truck alleys.

Here, licensing and robust health inspection limit liability and protect customers from foodborne illness, making street food in cities like Ottawa less organic and more sterile. The City of Ottawa's current approach to street food involves designated street vendor spaces. Former food reviewer Kathleen Walker once joked that street vendors are "regulated within an inch of their wagon wheels."

Accordingly, 1980s vendors were limited to selling "French fries, ice cream, soft drinks, sandwiches, hotdogs, cakes, cookies, doughnuts, coffee, subs, pogo sticks, elephant ears, tea, milk, hamburgers, soup, gum and candies, corn-on-the-cob, juices, egg rolls, fruits, vegetables, popcorn, and peanuts." Hot dog carts, of which there were 196 licensees, were limited to hot dogs, beverages and ice cream. Back then, vendors required a license to serve food, but there were no guidelines about where hot dog carts or chip trucks could set up for the day.

Bylaw amendments would ban vendors from retailing forty-six metres from a licensed restaurant with a customer seating area of thirty-seven square meters or less; ninety-one metres from public markets or on Sparks Street without permission; nine metres from intersections of the downtown core; sidewalk areas abutting malls; and north of Wellington Street in front of Parliament Hill and the Chateau Laurier. Then there were size restrictions for stands and carts.

Another bylaw, introduced in 1998, prevents vendors from selling anything between the hours of 1:00 a.m. and 5:00 a.m. Hot dog vendors and chip trucks used to congregate in the ByWard Market to specifically target people filing out of the bars and taverns after last call.

BITE THIS

One licensee, Donna Kyd, operated five hot dog carts, selling hot dogs and sausages with sautéed onions and peppers at the corner of Bank Street and Fourth Avenue in the Glebe neighbourhood. Kyd would go on to open one of the city's first modern "gourmet" food trucks, Bite This, in 2010. Renting an empty lot at the corner of Scott and McRae Streets in the Westboro neighbourhood, she parked her custom trailer on the gravel, set out some brightly coloured Muskoka chairs and pushed out fusion noodle bowls and her classic 6.5 oz "Big Honkin' Juicy" burger to crowds that grew each year. Bite This is known for its pad Thai ("Thai-One-On") and North American Chinese-inspired chow mein ("Momo-Chow-Wow"). Kyd would move Bite This to its permanent location at 179 Richmond Road three years later, directly across from a Loblaws Superstore. There she set up a weatherproof structure around her service window, protecting her customers from the elements when they order. Kyd owns the property.

For a time, vying for popular high-traffic spots in the city could lead to heated arguments or physical confrontations. Some vendors would camp out first thing in the morning to stake a claim. In 1996, a designated space program, modelled after the ByWard Market's, was implemented to address the issue. But with 120 on-street licenses already issued, a moratorium on new permit applications followed. The city reserved the right not to make vacant designated space available to new licensees. Existing permits could

Donna Kyd's Bite This food trailer in its original location at the corner of Scott and McRae in Westboro.

only be transferred to a spouse or family member. If vendors failed to renew their permits because they moved away or retired, their spots disappeared from the cityscape.

Andrew Lay of Sunnydays BBQ, who operated a blue-framed hot dog cart at the corner of Sparks and Bank starting in 1984, had to apply for a special stay of revocation. He planned to backpack through China. There, he would meet his wife and help her operate a restaurant. They returned with a seventeen-month-old baby in 2009. His permit would have lapsed otherwise. Over the years, Lay introduced a veggie dog and grilled chicken on a bun. Adding value to the lowly hot dog, customers could order off-the-menu freshly grilled vegetables as a topping. In 2014, Lay and his blue cart participated again as a Winterlude concession on the Rideau Canal. On the ice next to him was a shiny new food trailer, Sula Wok, operated by his wife. As he did brisk business selling hot dogs, she served Tibetan Momo dumplings to some enthusiastic skaters. The couple retrofitted and rebranded one of his former hot dog carts so they could sell Asian-inspired tacos on Bank Street in the summer of 2014. Toppings for the tacos include kale, apple slaw and green papaya salad.

During the moratorium, North American street food culture started emerging, becoming more visible, especially in traditional and new media (both television and online). But no new street food options appeared on public streets in Ottawa. Tensions between prospective street food entrepreneurs and the city festered. About seventy city-designated spaces disappeared by 2012.

Stone Soup Food Works

Some pioneers joined Donna Kyd. They moved ahead, outfitting trucks, trailers or carts and operating them on private property. There was Jacqueline Jolliffe of Stone Soup Food Works, who launched her truck at Winterlude in February 2011. Nicknamed "Sweet Pea," the green truck that started its life selling fries made its debut at the 4.4km mark (marked from the downtown start of the Rideau Canal) on the ice. Jolliffe's Stone Soup Food Works is named after the fable that tells of hungry strangers convincing townsfolk, during a time of scarcity, to contribute ingredients to a pot of soup that ends up being enjoyed by all. Former teacher, current food educator and passionate slow food advocate, Jolliffe is particularly concerned about serving people nourishing food. These past semesters, she and Sweet Pea have been parked at the University of Ottawa campus, serving soups (chowders, tomato soup and gazpachos), chilis (meat and vegetarian), salads (lentil salads, bean salads, couscous pilaf and nappa slaw carrot salads) and tacos (Korean steak with kimchi, pulled rosemary and honey pork, shredded beef and organic adobo chicken)—everything made from scratch. Some days she has been known to serve okonomiyaki, a kind of savoury Japanese pancake. Her ingredients are sourced from local producers like Grazing Days, Waratah Downs and Funny Duck Farms.

There was also Paul Bergeron of Relish the Flavour, who launched his blue truck at a street festival called Westfest in June 2012. An alumnus of Ottawa's Fraser Café, Bergeron dreamed of making restaurant-quality food mobile. With years spent on the line as a cook and sous, he decided to take fine dining to the streets. Like his friend Jolliffe, he, too, believes in quality ingredients, sourcing everything as locally as possible. You can also find him parked at the University of Ottawa campus, serving up his brand of atypical food truck food to students, staff and anyone else who happens by.

Past menus have included goat cheese arancini with mixed greens; butter chicken with rice; pork schnitzel sandwiches with coleslaw; beef tacos with truck-made tortillas; chicken curry salad sandwich with apple, red onion, cucumber and radish; and even doughnuts suspiciously reminiscent of the legendary ones his former chefs Simon and Ross Fraser serve in the Beechwood neighbourhood.

Trailer Pork Boys

Gerry Macies, Jennifer Demers and Rob and Adam Fata launched the former Trailer Pork Boys in July 2012. The trailer was quite the sight. Emblazoned with three porkers to the right of its two service windows, it was equipped with a complete commercial kitchen (refrigeration, fryolaters, ovens and flat top). A decidedly family affair, Adam Fata managed the truck initially with Chef Peter Simpson, both alumni from Caffe Mio. Rob Fata owns Caffe Mio (1379 Wellington Street West), a popular North American/Italian eatery located in the West Wellington Village. Macies owned the Best Western Hotel behind the truck and the corresponding land on which the truck was parked. Originally located at the corner of Carling and Merivale, Trailer Pork Boys served dishes based on authentic barbecue. "We had the bug," exclaimed Demers, Macies's wife. "We wanted to try our hand at a restaurant."[19]

The truck was the result of a confluence of talent. Macies provided recipes that he and Demers developed over the years as barbecue hobbyists. She is a communications professional and was the voice of the business. Rob Fata provided the restaurant expertise, helping with day-to-day operations, purchasing and managing food costs. Together they bought the trailer used, retrofitted it and customized it, adding a commercial smoker. "Ours was a partnership. Street food is a cash business. You have to maintain a level of trust between you, your partners and staff. The key is to have [well] defined roles."

Trailer Pork Boys was known for its pulled pork, which went into everything. Besides straight sandwiches, it went into "Cubans" and grilled cheese. Its flagship product, the pulled pork was made over two days. Accordingly, pork butt (shoulder) was dry-rubbed, smoked, transferred to a pan and roasted with apple juice and dressed in scratch barbecue sauce. The Cuban was an enormous sandwich made with the pulled pork, sliced ham, sliced dills, Swiss cheese and Southwest-style sauce. Realizing that they needed to offer a pulled pork–free alternative, the truck also served a schnitzel sandwich. "We kept a short and efficient menu," explained Demers. "Ottawa shows incredible enthusiasm for street food, but the trucks have to deliver. We could not let our customers wait an hour for their food."

After three successful years operating the truck, Macies sold the hotel. Everyone went their separate ways. "It's actually a lot of fun if you are willing to work hard," he said. "Lesson learned? Maintain constant communications. Word of mouth will only go so far."

THE FLAT BREAD PIZZA COMPANY

Mark Snyder of the Flat Bread Pizza Company started doing events in 2011. Formerly an accomplished commercial photographer, Snyder decided to follow his dream of preparing and serving wood-fired pizza on the go. More of a cart-style operation, his Flat Bread Pizza Company can be found set up at indoor and outdoor festivals. He used to be a fixture at the Ottawa Farmers' Market at Brewer Park. Presently, he sets up every weekend at a cycling shop just outside the Beechwood neighbourhood. Like most food trucks and carts, he caters private events as well.

"We do a lot of private events. I adore catering. It allows me to be creative and ensure my guests get a quality product. I have no intention of doing street side [vending]. It's a different challenge. I'm not set up for it,"[20] explained Snyder.

"I like to get my hands into everything from working the dough…to chopping the [meat]…to cleaning the oven. You need to maintain quality! Quality for pizza involves how the dough is handled, heat of the oven and time the pizza spends in the oven. I'm constantly tinkering."

Snyder's branded mobile oven, which requires a custom trailer to lug around, produces Neapolitan-style artisanal pizzas that showcase innovative combinations of toppings, many borrowing from classical pizzas: san marzano tomatoes, fresh garlic, oregano and extra virgin olive oil; oven-roasted fennel sausage, scallions, purple onions, organic panna and mozzarella; salami, purple onions, black olives and mozzarella; mixed mushrooms (cremini, shiitake, porcini), smoked mozzarella and herb oil;

Mark Snyder of the Flat Bread Pizza Company bakes pizzas to order in his mobile wood-fired oven.

and Mariposa duck confit (local farmer), wine-poached pears, caramelized onions and Canreg Station St. Laurent blue (a local cheese).

"When I'm set up, I offer three pizzas. One tends to be vegetarian, sometimes vegan. The second usually appeals to meat eaters. The third is the 'interesting' one, something original. It's always unpredictable how the general public will receive the 'wacky' pizza."

When requested, he will prepare the classic margherita as well: san marzano tomatoes, buffalo mozzarella, fresh basil and extra virgin olive oil. He also makes calzones: Tuscan wild boar stew with Parmigiano-Reggiano; oven-roasted mushrooms with porcini, truffle oil and buffalo mozzarella; and maplewood-grilled Tamworth Italian sausage stew with onions, peppers and mozzarella.

With new trucks, trailers and carts venturing into the market, participating as concessions for events like festivals and concerts, signing up as food vendors at farmers' markets and catering, the City of Ottawa took notice of the increased profile and buzz around street food.

"For the first time in twenty years, we had to find new [spaces] for [street] vendors. But how do we ensure the food will be fresh and healthy?"

explained Philip Powell, manager of licensing, permits and markets for the City of Ottawa. "The one-size-fit-nobody [à la cart] program in Toronto didn't work."

The City of Ottawa, under Mayor Jim Watson, realized that the moratorium on space permits had reduced the number of street food vendors over the past two decades to forty-four. Ottawa wanted more ethnically diverse street fare than hot dogs, fries and poutine. Thereafter, city council would approve the "New Street Food Vendor Program," offering twenty on-street spaces to applicants that best met selection criteria established by a "Street Food Selection Panel."

"The new [spaces] had to be forty-six metres away from an existing food premise. They had to be approved by the Ward Councillor and Business Improvement Area (BIA)," Powell noted. Applicants had to submit a proposal with a business plan, menu and any supplemental information they thought would persuade the selection panel. The panel was made up of representatives from the Ontario Restaurant, Hotel & Motel Association (ORHMA); the Ottawa branch of the Canadian Culinary Federation (CCF); Savour Ottawa; Just Food; and Public Health. "The existing licensees could keep their [spaces]. They were not allowed to select a new [space] unless they changed their menu [and applied to the same process as new prospective vendors]."

Of the sixty-one application received, seventeen (ten trucks and seven carts) were approved by the panel in February 2013 and invited to apply for licenses, according to Powell. "The panellists couldn't believe the quality of the applications. Ben Baird [of Streat Food Gourmet] submitted an amazing plan. Applications were scored numerically. [Spaces] were assigned based on scores."

As before, new vendors require licenses that demonstrate that their trucks or carts are suitable to serve food. This includes a Technical Standards & Safety Authority (TSSA) safety "check" (inspection and approval) and a health "check." The fee for a one-year license is $3,600 and does not include the TSSA inspection fee.

The fee for a one-year space permit is $4,000, which affords the permit holder the right to vend in the associated location during specific hours of the day. However, recognizing that Ottawa spends several months under a thick blanket of snow and ice, a six-month permit is available. The fee amount represents the average revenue lost in parking fees since a truck or cart will be occupying the location.

While incumbent vendors were approved, many struggled to roll out their operations due to unforeseen complications in coming months. Due to increased demand for street food, food truck and cart manufacturers and mobile food service equipment vendors were inundated with orders not just from Ottawa but also from across the country. This resulted in production delays. Some vendors also had significant difficulty navigating the requirements set out by the licenses to demonstrate that their rigs were safe to operate. Others were unfamiliar with the day-to-day operations of a food service business. "We watched the new program's vendors with rapt attention. It took us a year to get Trailer Pork Boys up and running," said Demers.

One year later, of the incumbent seventeen food trucks and carts, two had stopped operating on the street. Jolliffe's Stone Soup Food Works opted to concentrate on catering and private events. She is also involved in newly launched the West End Well (969 Wellington Street West), a cooperative grocery store in Hintonburg. Jolliffe will run its café. LeRoy H. Walden Jr., the former proprietor of Jean Albert's, a brick-and-mortar restaurant on Somerset Street West (495), sold his "Detroit Style Soul Food" truck and purchased commercial space on Gladstone Avenue (707), opening a new restaurant. There, he's back to serving up American fare like fried chicken and waffles. "The truck just wasn't for me," explained Walden.

Those surviving program incumbent trucks and carts retail a variety of street food, including Korean bibimbap (bap), Southern Indian Dosas, Asian fusion rice and noodle bowls, Chinese steamed buns and sustainable fish and chips and lobster rolls.

bap by Raon Kitchen

Raon Kitchen is the brainchild of Hana Jung, a marketing manager, and her husband, Iruk Cho, a web designer (and recent graduate from the culinary program at Algonquin College). They moved to Ottawa from Seoul, South Korea, with their young daughter nearly five years ago.

Their popular bap on Bank Street is one of the incumbent food carts. Raon Kitchen has, in fact, been in business for two summers, selling its kimchi (fermented napa cabbage) and marinades such as ganjang (a Korean soy sauce) and gochujang (a chili pepper paste) at the Main Farmers' Market on Saturdays, as well as at the Ottawa Farmers' Market on Saturdays in Westboro and Sundays in Brewer Park.

Staff at bap by Raon Kitchen during the Ottawa Street Food Launch Event at City Hall. On the right is founder Iruk Cho.

Bibimbap from the bap cart by Raon Kitchen. Beef bibimbap (left) and spicy chicken bibimbap (right).

Jung and Cho's passion for using local and quality ingredients to make great food is obvious. It has something to do with their eating as locally as possible. Cho explained, "Eating local isn't new…Koreans are obsessed with the idea of 'Sintoburi,' which means our body and the land are not separate literally. In short, domestic farm products are the best for our health."

Since opening their food cart last June, bap by Raon Kitchen has amassed a following. It's not unusual to find a lineup of patrons hungry for Korea's signature dish, "bibimbap." Normally bibimbap is served as a rice bowl topped with sautéed vegetables, gochujang, slices of meat and either a raw egg yolk or runny fried egg.

Unfortunately, since bap is a food cart, prep has to be done off-site and ahead of time. So it is somewhat difficult to offer a raw or runny fried egg option. However, you will find spinach, thinly sliced Korean-style egg omelettes, julienned carrots, daikon radishes, bell peppers and shiitake mushrooms. For protein, you can choose between beef, spicy chicken or tofu.

Angry Dragonz

Angry Dragonz on Gloucester Street, another incumbent food truck, is run by the husband-and-wife team of Kin Tran and Bonnie Wong. Food has always been a big part of their lives, especially for Tran, having worked in the restaurant industry for years and having previously owned several restaurants, including Asia River on River Road, Koi Asia in Bells Corners and China Hut on Sparks Street.

Offering "Asian fusion with a twist," they sell Hong Kong–style snacks of egg puffs, which they top and pass off as waffles. This snack is hugely popular in Chinatown and in Asian malls in Toronto and Vancouver.

On the savoury side, they sell grilled skewers of lamb, beef and chicken, as well as tofu. The chicken skewers are marinated with a sweet tamarind sauce. The lamb is coated in cumin and sprinkled with chili and garlic. The bulgogi beef in their bibimbap rice box is marinated in a Korean-style barbecue sauce and served with fresh veggies. It can be served topped with a fried egg. The pad Thai noodle bowl is made with a tamarind sauce and is served with chicken, fresh vegetables and egg.

One of the more prolific food trucks, Tran and Wong participate in many events on the summer festival circuit.

GONGFU BAO

One of the most anticipated of the incumbent food trucks was Gongfu Bao by Tarek Hassan. After months of delays, Hassan triumphantly drove his newly manufactured, customized and inspected Gongfu Bao cart to its location on Elgin Street, across from the Lord Elgin Hotel (100 Elgin Street).

Firstly, he crowd-funded almost $6,000 via Indiegogo to purchase his cart from Vancouver manufacturer Apollo. The campaign ended on May 19, 2013. Then Hassan had to work with the back-ordered manufacturer to produce and ship the cart. Afterward, he had to work with the various powers-that-be to repeatedly demonstrate that his cart was safe for food service.

Hassan, a former line cook and Carleton University engineering graduate, makes Chinese char siu barbecue pork from heritage pork (usually Berkshire) and pressed tofu for his take on what he refers to as the "original" street food, steamed buns.

Contrary to local culinary urban legend, there was no pivotal moment when he ventured into the world of steamed buns. Hassan can't seem to remember when he first encountered them. "It was either at [a Toronto] T&T or at the freezer section of a supermarket," explained Hassan.

An alumnus of Fraser Café, Sidedoor, former Savannah Café and Izakaya, he lists chefs Michael Radford and Jonny Korecki as mentors, having adopted their food philosophies. When it comes to food, Hassan likens cooking to martial arts—a balance of careful technique and ingredients produces flavour and texture. He learned his "pleating" technique from a Tibetan monk. Regarding ingredients, Hassan believes that food must be sourced well but priced so it can be accessible to anyone. While he prefers to cook with ingredients sourced from local farms, he employs Oriental cooking techniques and flavour profiles.

Served up with a multi-textured slaw, some of Hassan's more classic bao includes his maple char siu bao; pork belly guo bao; Shanghai grilled cheese with leek, brown butter and tomato soup "demi-glace" bao; and curried chickpea bao. For events and catering, he makes one-offs like "jerked" chickpea and butternut squash bao and char sui and golden sag paneer. During Winterlude, he innovated a breakfast bao, a tamarind and coconut rolled "cinna-Bao."

Lunch

Tim Van Dyke's brick-and-mortar locations and food truck called Lunch serve socially conscious meals that are healthy and delicious, competitively priced (under ten dollars for sandwich and soup or salad combos) and "prêt à manger." "Our goal is for people [we serve] to be eating a good, honest and fresh product,"[21] he explained.

In 2013, before his retrofitted food truck became one of the incumbents, he and his staff were already serving 1,000 people a day. This worked out to between 250 and 400 cubicle dwellers, dropping into each location during their lunch breaks. Recently, Van Dyke expanded into Gatineau with a Lunch location in the causeway connecting the office towers that make up the third phase of the enormous office complex Place du Portage (PDP3).

Lunch celebrated its sixth anniversary on April 16, 2014. It originally opened on Bank Street (121), between Slater and Albert Streets. Van Dyke's now flagship retail outlet once produced all of the food served at his satellite locations. It is the only one equipped with a kitchen, but it has no gas line. He and his former chef Alex Majpaniw worked with electric hot plates and portable induction burners. These days, all the sandwiches, soups and salads served at 121 Bank, 99 Metcalfe, 240 Sparks and Place du Portage are assembled at the "commissary," a central professionally equipped kitchen in Chinatown (60-A Lebreton).

"Best selling? The chicken tarragon salad sandwich. It's a classic chicken salad," he noted. For his food truck, Van Dyke retrofitted a 1995 Chevrolet P30 to be a mobile retail location, serving the same menu as any other Lunch outlet. When parked, a diesel generator powers the refrigeration he needs.

Local "metal artist" Alan Gustafson did the "heavy lifting." Graffiti artist Luke Norrad hand-painted the logo onto the truck, sort of a typographic mural. The service window measures four by eleven feet, the average dimensions of the signature chalkboards at Lunch's various locations.

Tim Van Dyke's Lunch food truck.

In November 2014, the city will undergo its first-year review of the street food program. This could involve a call for possible new locations and having vendors swap spaces. Also, with ground already broken for the construction of the new light rail system, Phillip Powell and city council want to work with the public transit commission and transit services (OC Transpo) to look into spaces for trucks and carts.

The city's complement of food trucks and carts, some operating on public streets and others on private property, have been vending a number of years now. Operators have learned some harsh lessons.

For program incumbents, the stationary space permits proved restrictive, preventing vendors from following foot traffic. They couldn't shift to wherever there will be higher concentrations of people during the day or evening. Moreover, with respect to downtown spaces, weekend traffic patterns differ from weekday ones. Many locations are so quiet that it has not been cost effective to open Saturdays or Sundays.

There is limited privately owned property from which to operate a food truck or cart. Many spaces are already spoken for. Landlords are wary of renting to food trucks, sometimes due to power and garbage disposal requirements.

Street food is extremely weather dependent. In poor weather (high heat, high humidity or rain), few patrons will venture out, preferring brick-and-mortar restaurants. Most venders have not been able to operate in the winter, so they needed to consider alternative income for six to eight months of the year.

Festivals are not cash cows. Concession rental space can be very costly. Many festivals restrict operators to one or two dishes to prevent competition amongst concessions. If the weather is too warm, festivalgoers simply will not eat. Moreover, during Winterlude, festivalgoers will opt for cheaper fries, poutine and pop.

Confrontations between vendors and surrounding brick-and-mortar businesses, especially food service operations, have become commonplace and increasingly bitter. The Sparks Street Business Improvement Area directing street food vendors to stop selling ready-made food products in May 2014 was one of the more public examples. Vendors signed agreements with the Sparks Street Mall to sell products at its farmers' market. Surrounding restaurants, cafés and pubs saw the vendors as competition.

Roadwork and construction turn away prospective patrons whether you are a café with a patio or a food truck or cart.

Repaying debt generated by investing in street food equipment has been slow. Food trucks can cost as much as luxury apartment condominiums.

As a result, street food operators have gathered and created an association, the Capital Street Food Association. It allows them to better articulate concerns with city officials. At the meetings, they also discuss challenges with event organizers and leverage one another's experience. Its current president is Mario Burke of the Ad Mare Seafood Truck. Burke is a program incumbent, operating at the corner of Slater and O'Connor Streets, and previous licensee, formerly operating three canteen trucks.

Chapter 7

WE TAKE CARE OF OUR OWN

Nothing could be worse than the fear that one had given up too soon, and left one unexpended effort that might have saved the world.
–Jane Addams, activist, author, community organizer and leader in women's suffrage

Although Jane Addams's message was for women in the late 1800s and early 1900s, it remains relevant to this day. We are all responsible for making our communities better places to live. Although we are fortunate to live in a society that is well off, there are many who find themselves in less favourable circumstances.

Food nourishes, sustains and supplies the human body and mind. Sustenance is required as we push through each day. And yet such a basic need often goes unfulfilled for many. Hunger is prevalent in many low-income families in many cities across North America, including here in the nation's capital.

But ours is a caring community. Many in the food and restaurant industry have dedicated themselves to improving the lives of others. It is through their efforts, generosity and contributions that local programs execute their missions. When it comes to taking care of those who are most vulnerable, look no further than the Ottawa Food Bank.

OTTAWA FOOD BANK

To the Ottawa Food Bank, hunger erodes "human dignity, lessens human energy and impairs potential." The organization has been helping to fight community hunger since 1984, when it started in the basement of a former police station on Waller Street. Initially a temporary measure, it eventually became a staple food relief organization in the region. Today, the Ottawa Food Bank supports 140 emergency food programs that feed about forty-eight thousand people per month, with 37 percent of those being children.

The mission of the Ottawa Food Bank is to collect and distribute food to member agencies serving people in need in the Ottawa area. Such agencies include schools, emergency shelters and community food banks. Its vision is to ensure that no one goes hungry.

Patti Murphy, director of communications and development, and Sarah Burns, event manager, have worked at the Ottawa Food Bank for about five years. There is enthusiasm and pride in their voices as they describe the work of the food bank. In 2012, the Ottawa Food Bank distributed 7,224,741 pounds of food, with more than three thousand volunteers having donated 21,031 hours. But it is the relationships with their chefs, restaurants and farmers and their meat programs that have them most excited. "We have a great partnership with local chefs,"[22] said Murphy. Within the past three years, Ottawa Food Bank has partnered with more than a dozen restaurants, many locally owned. Union Local 613 is currently donating profits from its Monday lunch and clothing sales, while Fiazza Fresh Fired is donating money from gift card sales to a fund that supports the Ottawa Food Bank along with two other charities. Over the years, partner restaurants have helped raise thousands of dollars.

The Ottawa Food Bank's partnership with farmers, Murphy and Burns proudly explained, has also been a real success. Nearly four years ago, the Ottawa Food Bank embarked on a pilot project chosen by the Ontario Association of Food Banks to partner with local farmers in order to dramatically increase the amount of fresh, healthy produce distributed through their member agencies and, in turn, local families in need. "We are working on developing a strong network of local farmers who can set aside land for growing projects," Burns stated. Both immediately brought up Tom Black, whose farm is located in Stittsville. In turn, Ottawa Food Bank volunteers help prepare beds, plant seeds, weed and pick produce, and the farm donates leftover produce that cannot be sold at markets. The volunteers, Murphy noted, include families, students and employees from businesses that have also formed partnerships with the Ottawa Food Bank.

With the Black family generously donating four acres of land for the 2014 growing season, Ottawa Food Bank has planted a variety of vegetables, including potatoes, cabbage, beets, carrots and zucchini. Jason Gray, the community harvest coordinator, has been instrumental in the planting. "Jason determines what to plant and what is needed. He works sixty to seventy hours a week. When the growing season is over, he is pretty exhausted," Murphy ended with a laugh. According to Gray, by the end of the 2013 growing season, the project had yielded 53,561 pounds of fruit and vegetables (a 257 percent increase over 2012) and engaged 477 volunteers for a total of 1,423 hours.

Regarding nearby farms, Murphy and Burns explained, "We [also] receive donations from other area farmers and have gleaning opportunities. Last year, we gleaned at Foster Family Farm, Proulx, Sugarbush and Berry Farm and Needham's Market Garden." Apples and corn were some of the late summer and fall crops harvested from the farms. In addition, the Ottawa Food Bank is also set up at the Ottawa Farmers' Market. Noting the generous donations from the vendors there, Burns proudly recalled that in 2013 alone, they received 10,880 pounds of food. "Our farmers are incredibly generous," Murphy pointed out and further explained that all the fresh fruits and vegetables have made a real difference in helping families get access to fresh food they normally cannot afford.

Another long-running and unique program is the Ground Beef Program. As far as Murphy and Burns are aware, it may be the only program of its kind in Canada. At the height of the mad cow disease crisis in 2003, prices for beef fell sharply, and Canadians consumed less, despite only a reported single case of a lone cow with Bovine Spongiform Encephalitis (BSE) on a remote northern Alberta farm. Countries like the United States, Japan and Mexico closed their borders to Canadian beef. That is when the Ottawa Food Bank came up with the ingenious idea to form a relationship with local beef farmers. "We wanted to help the farmers, and they get to help the Food Bank. Since the cost of beef was so low, we were able to purchase a lot," Burns stated. From June 2005 to April 30, 2014, 1,757 cows were purchased, with 204 cows donated. Based on the last 15 cows purchased and/or processed, the average hung weight of one cow was 647 pounds. To date, an average of 361 pounds of ground beef has been received per cow. It is astonishing that 878,459 pounds of ground beef has already been distributed. The average cost of one cow at a livestock barn was $1,345.00, with $672,921.99 in total abattoir processing charges paid thus far. A constant supply of fresh ground beef reflects the unique rural-urban partnership between farmers and the Food Bank but also provides inexpensive and nutritious fresh meat for those in need.

Other food partnerships crucial to the Ottawa Food Bank include the Egg Farmers of Canada, occasionally the Turkey Farmers of Canada and its current relationship with the Chicken Farmers of Canada. With the addition of its initiative with the Chicken Farmers of Canada, the Ottawa Food Bank is now able to distribute more animal protein to its beneficiaries than ever before. On Canada Day, an annual barbecue from Chicken Farmers on Parliament Hill regularly raises thousands of dollars for the fight against community hunger. In 2010, $50,000 worth of frozen chicken was purchased. Each quarter, the Food Bank receives a new stock of frozen chicken that is then distributed to its agencies. Nowadays, the chickens are generally whole, although there is sometimes processed chicken.

Murphy and Burns feel honoured that food banks across Canada look to the Ottawa Food Bank as an example for its innovative programs and eagerness to share information. Asked what they hope to see in the future, they immediately replied:

> *We hope that someday we will no longer exist. It's a dream, but we still hope. There's a wonderful movement from businesses, a wonderful energy with food. There is so much choice now. People are starting to want to know where their* [food comes from]. *Farmers are looking after the locals, taking care of our community.* [Our clients] *are not their regular customers but still need caring. We hope to continue working with local farmers, continue our partnerships and grow them. We hope to keep planting more at Black Farm and purchase fresh food throughout the year.*

PARKDALE FOOD CENTRE

Over a cup of coffee at a nearby coffee shop, Karen Secord asked, "Did you know there are fourteen rooming houses in the neighbourhood?"[23] It is seemingly contradictory, this need for a food bank in an area of town under siege by gentrification. Mechanicsville butts up against Hintonburg, the formerly bohemian younger sibling of affluent West Wellington Village and Westboro. Now Hintonburg has one of the highest densities of restaurants in Ottawa. With all available land in the area being purchased and developed into high-rise condominium complexes, housing prices have soared.

But like any neighbourhood, there lies another story behind the gloss. Secord, executive director of Parkdale Food Centre, runs an organization that provides emergency food aid to individuals and families in need. A subsidiary of the Ottawa Food Bank, tenants represent nearly 60 percent of clients to the Parkdale Centre, with the rest coming from family shelters and transition houses. Proud of the operation she runs out of space rented from a Russian Orthodox church in Mechanicsville, she explained, "We [also] feed families you wouldn't expect to [need to] visit a food bank. Everyone is welcome. We don't judge!"

Parkdale Food Centre's mission is to provide healthy food, nutrition education and a warm and welcoming environment to neighbours in need. Secord has worked hard to establish the healthy food component of the mission. "Did you know generous donors sponsor 'Good Food Boxes' for our clients?" she asked. Of the two dozen or so monthly CSA-style (Community Supported Agriculture) boxes of fruits and vegetables that arrive monthly at the Centre for nearby homeowners, half a dozen or so are sponsored for clients, mostly families. Unable to afford fresh produce at grocery stores, these boxes are in some respects lifesavers for these families. Nearby elementary schools also keep vegetable gardens and donate the produce to Parkdale Food Centre to distribute.

Not your average food bank coordinator, Secord pioneered a number of innovative initiatives since taking the volunteer role in 2012. She is working to upend long-held assumptions about food banks. For instance, she refuses to stock "better than nothing" food like Kraft Dinner or chicken wieners. "Someone donated a pallet of bubble gum," she said, exasperated.

Instead, hers is a very different distribution system of whole foodstuffs. The Centre's pantries, freezers and fridges are packed with staples from bread to eggs, chicken legs, ground beef, flour, sugar, salt, canned tomatoes, canned fish, instant coffee, potatoes, onions, beets, carrots and apples. There is also toothpaste, soap, laundry detergent, razors, shampoo, deodorant and toilet paper.

Secord also partners with nearby restaurants, caterers, fine food shops and even local microbrewery Beyond the Pale for donations and fundraising.

Thyme and Again, a fine food shop and catering business, and newly opened Zazaza have been particularly generous of late. Neighbourhood volunteers, including those from nearby restaurant businesses, come in Tuesday evenings to bake bran muffins to distribute.

Accordingly, Secord works to break the cycle of poverty by limiting access to heavily processed foods. They saddle already disadvantaged people with health problems that stem from diets low in nutrition but high in calories. Obesity, for instance, tends to lead to diabetes. The World Health Organization (WHO) describes food security as built on three pillars. Firstly, food availability means sufficient quantities of food available on a consistent basis. Secondly, food access refers to having sufficient resources to obtain appropriate foods for a nutritious diet. Thirdly, food use is defined as appropriate use based on knowledge of basic nutrition and care, as well as adequate water and sanitation. To address the oft-forgotten third pillar, Secord organizes cooking classes with guest instructors at the end of each month. Classes are exclusive to clients. Instructors to date have included chefs of local restaurants and a food editor of an Ottawa magazine.

According to the WHO, besides food availability and accessibility, "appropriate use" is critical. Essentially, having foodstuffs is not enough. People require an understanding of how to feed themselves, so nutrition and care are important. This means basic cooking skills. Thus, attendees of Secord's mostly demonstration-based cooking classes leave with crockpots, recipes and ingredients to re-create dishes at home. She added that her classes also foster community. Poverty carries stigma. For some attendees, the class is one of few excursions out. The vast majority have not eaten a family-style meal in recent memory.

Operating in the community bordered by Bayswater Avenue, Carling Avenue, Island Park Drive and the Ottawa River, it is a small geographic area. Yet this not-for-profit charity provides emergency food assistance for about 700 people per month, with 150 of those being children.

In December 2013, Karen Secord's tireless efforts were recognized when she received the Mayor's City Builder Award for her outstanding community service. The centre's clients and also the community have benefited from her dedication, as Parkdale Food Centre has become a model for other community food banks and centres.

The Ottawa Mission

Food banks have made enormous contributions to the community and food scene. One organization that has served the city for more than a century is the Ottawa Mission.

Established in 1906, the Ottawa Mission has been propelled by Christian spirit. The original founders, a group of Christian businessmen, wanted to help other men facing difficult times. Food, shelter and, when available, clothing were provided. They were motivated by the desire to help those who did not have the resources to help themselves. This spirit continues to conduct the Mission well into the twenty-first century.

Over the years, the Mission's clients have sought help for various reasons, including family breakdown, addiction, physical and mental health problems, shortage of affordable housing and unemployment. While the Mission remains a shelter for homeless men, women can access its hospice nursing beds, community meals and an array of client and medical services. Otherwise, women are referred to female-only shelters.

Not surprisingly, the biggest need at the Mission is food. The kitchen serves an average of 1,295 meals per day. Meals are served to more than two hundred residents of the shelter, as well as to many who live in the community. These people often have little money for food. Managing the food services is Chef Ric Watson. Having been a part of the Ottawa Mission for more than a decade, his story is rather remarkable.

Watson identifies with the clients, as he was once homeless, living on the streets at the age of fourteen. At sixteen, a food service company in Kingston, called Beaver Foods, hired him as a dishwasher. There, he worked his way up to become a cook's helper and a cook apprentice. Beaver Foods saw potential in him and so paid for his training and education. Watson earned his chef's papers and the Red Seal designation and went on to earn a hotel and restaurant management diploma. But rather than heading off to work in a restaurant like so many young chefs, Chef Watson chose a different path.

He can be found in the Mission kitchen by 5:00 a.m., cooking, directing and motivating staff and volunteers to ensure that more than 1,200 healthy meals are ready to be served. All soups and sauces are made from scratch. Holiday dinners are often reported on by local press, explaining the hours and volunteers required to feed more than two thousand of Ottawa's working poor and homeless. Outside the kitchen, Watson is also tasked with negotiating for donations of food and sponsorships to help keep costs as low as possible. For example, in 2006, he made arrangements with the Chateau Laurier (formerly known as the Fairmont Chateau Laurier) in which the hotel would donate surplus food. Baked goods, yogurt, sandwiches, fruit and cut meats in pristine condition are just some of the surplus food. Oftentimes, food is left over from a banquet or buffet, untouched and prepared fresh daily. Special items like croissants are items the Mission normally would not have. Rather than throwing the food out, having it go to the Mission means that the shelter has a continuous supply of food.

The satisfaction in knowing that he is making a difference in people's lives has kept Watson coming back to work. Now with more than thirty years of experience in the food service industry, he also founded an in-house cook apprenticeship program that is unique to Ottawa shelters. The program aims to help people get out of homelessness by providing education. The hands-on training requires six months to complete. Now affiliated with Ontario Works, a provincial program that provides financial and employment assistance, graduates have gone on to the culinary program at Algonquin College. Watson has called his work in the program tiring and challenging but rewarding. The knowledge that participants want to succeed, get off social assistance and have the opportunity to give back to the Mission means everything to Watson. As part of his biography on the Mission's website, he is quoted as saying, "Many of the people we serve meals to are regulars, and I get to know a lot of them. I know that they have potential, just as I did, and I know they will do well if someone believes in them and gives them a chance."

His efforts have not gone unnoticed by his peers. In June 2014, Watson was the recipient of the Canadian Culinary Federation "Chef of the Year" award.

It takes a group of special and dedicated people willing to tackle issues of hunger in the community head on. Hours of hard work, building relationships with the public, farmers, restaurateurs and other businesses in the food industry are required. Compassion, respect, sacrifice and determination are needed in organizations striving to solve this complex issue.

Chapter 8

LOOKING TO THE FUTURE

When Canadian culinary cuisine is discussed, Ottawa is often overlooked in favour of larger metropolitan centres like Montreal, Toronto and Vancouver. A history of being a gastronomic wasteland, along with a stereotype of being boring, cemented our reputation as forgettable. However, Ottawa has worked hard over the years to shed this unfortunate image. The food scene in the nation's capital may still be relatively young, but it has developed immensely during the last thirty years.

When the second millennium came to pass, Ottawa saw rebirth, growth and proliferation. Immigration brought new ethnic options, food shops and eateries. Most importantly, immigration brought new attitudes and ideas. No longer are diners restricted to continental cuisine. We discovered other cultures' dishes, spices, flavours and textures. Even local practitioners of French cuisine changed, taking cues from around the world. Nouvelle cuisine encouraged chefs to look at seasonally available ingredients, taking into consideration regionally specific meat and produce. Dishes are lighter, focusing on ingredients.

The presence of Le Cordon Bleu and the highly respected culinary program at Algonquin College have attracted a legion of Canadian and international students. Many stay on in Ottawa. As they work their way up the line in the professional kitchen, their enthusiasm and youth spill onto diners' plates. We can taste their passion. The restaurant scene has exploded with thousands of options.

The late Kurt Waldele served Canadian cuisine to statesmen, dignitaries and celebrities. He demonstrated that taking a simple but skilled approach to Canadian ingredients from coast to coast can inspire. His legacy lives on, having mentored many chefs who still cook in Ottawa.

Ottawans are going back to their roots, rediscovering the rich offerings of eating and buying locally. By eating the "fruits" of the region, we are reconnecting with farmers and producers.

Craft beer is flowing freely, with breweries such as Kichesippi eager to showcase beer that is unique to the region. Never has the local beer scene been as exciting as it is now. With the promise of new breweries opening in the near future, beer drinkers can imagine the ancient Greek gods Silenus and Dionysus smiling down from the heavens.

And yet Ottawa finds itself at a crossroad. Not too long ago, Ottawa was selected as a possible culinary destination. Are we there yet? We have all the building blocks, from award-winning restaurants to producer-only farmers' markets, culinary schools and craft breweries. There is an emerging food truck scene. We have the ability to take care of our own. We live in a city in which 80 percent of the land is rural, resulting in nearly 1,200 farms. This is our foundation from which Ottawa can build anew.

Regional cuisines are dear to travellers who want to understand the culture one taste at a time. Diners must decide if they can identify with their food scene, distinguishing it from the rest of the country. Ottawa has all the potential to set itself apart and write a new chapter in its food history. Over a beer, Executive Chef Jason Duffy of ARC Lounge concluded his thoughts of the nation's capital: "Chefs are so creative in Ottawa. Wherever you go, it's an adventure. [Ottawa] is the best food city in Canada, but people just don't know that yet." As the city marches on into the future, we are excited to see what will develop. Only time will tell.

NOTES

Chapter 1

1. Paul Couvrette, photographer of Couvrette Studio, interview and discussion with the authors, May 14, 2014.
2. Charles Beauregarde, restaurateur of Canvas Resto-Bar, interview and discussion with the authors, April 26, 2014.
3. Eugene Haslam, owner of Zaphod Beeblebrox, interview and discussion with the authors, February 9, 2014.
4. Richard Nigro, owner of Richard's Kitchen, interview and discussion with the authors, June 30, 2014.
5. George Monsour, restaurateur of Back Lane Café, interview and discussion with the authors, May 25, 2014.
6. Pat Nicastro, owner/founder of La Bottega Nicastro, interview and discussion with the authors, June 23, 2014.
7. Kym Ng, manager of Yangtze Dining Lounge, interview and discussion with the authors, June 17, 2014.
8. Jason Duffy, executive chef of ARC Lounge at ARC The Hotel, interview and discussion with the authors, June 20, 2014.
9. Jose Bento and Madan Sharma, cooks of National Arts Centre, interview and discussion with the authors, May 22, 2014.
10. Phillippe Dupuy, former owner/chef of Le Saint-Ô, interview and discussion with the authors, July 10, 2014.

CHAPTER 2

11. Philip Powell, Markets Managements City of Ottawa, interview and discussion with the authors, June 10, 2014.

CHAPTER 3

12. Giuliano Boselli, former owner of Mamma Teresa, interview and discussion with the authors, May 14, 2014.
13. Craig Buckley, co-founder/owner of Kettleman's Bagel Co., interview and discussion with the authors, May 14, 2014.
14. Marysol Foucault, chef/owner of Edgar, interview and discussion with the authors, March 2014.

CHAPTER 4

15. Stephen Beckta, owner of Beckta Dining, Play Food & Wine, Gezelling, interview and discussion with the authors, June 3, 2014.
16. Kyle Mortimer-Proulx, chef of Lowertown Brewery, interview and discussion with the authors, April 12, 2014.

CHAPTER 5

17. Paul Meek, owner/founder of Kichisippi Beer Co., interview and discussion with the authors, May 27, 2014.
18. Shane Clark and Rob McIssac, founders of Beyond the Pale, interview and discussion with the authors, June 26, 2014.

Chapter 6

19. Jennifer Demers, Trailer Pork Boys, interview and discussion with Don, August 2012.
20. Mark Snyder, owner of Flatbread Pizza Co., interview and discussion with the authors, June 2014.
21. Tim Van Dyke, owner of Lunch, interview and discussion with the authors, April 2013.

Chapter 7

22. Patti Murphy and Sarah Burns, the Ottawa Food Bank, interview and discussion with the authors, July 7, 2014.
23. Karen Secord, Parkdale Food Centre, executive director, interview and discussion with the authors, September 16, 2013.

BIBLIOGRAPHY

À La Carte. "William Street Café's Greek Salad Delicious." Ottawa: Ottawa Citizen, March 31, 1993.

Anderson, Mark. "Burger King: The Man Behind Ottawa's Hit Hamburger Chain, the Works." *Ottawa Citizen*, April 13, 2007. www.canada.com/story.html?id=f05801f4-e4dc-47d9-896a-fcdd7d868d33.

Atherton, Tony. "The Chinatown Dream; Not Everyone Favors Making Somerset an 'Oriental Midway.'" *Ottawa Citizen*, August 16, 1986.

Barth, Willy. "Six Brothers and a Dream Built Nicastro Food Stores." *Ottawa Citizen*, May 12, 1979.

Bohuslawsky, Maria. "Midas Touch or Kiss of Death? Ottawa's Vision for the ByWard Market Evicts Some Longtime Tenants." *Ottawa Citizen*, March 16, 1995.

———. "Parkdale Market Celebrates Deep Roots." *Ottawa Citizen*, July 11, 1994.

Bowering, Ian. *The Art and Mystery of Brewing in Ontario*. Burnstown, ON: General Store Publishing House Inc., 1988.

Canada's Who's Who 2002. "Waldele, Kurt." Vol. 37. Toronto: University of Toronto Press, 2002.

Canadian Tourism Commission. "China." http://en-corporate.canada.travel/research/market-knowledge/china.

Chianello, Joanne. "ByWard Is in a Crisis; City's Beloved Market Needs a Vision and a Feasible Plan." *Ottawa Citizen*, August 8, 2013.

———. "City Hall Should Loosen Up; Street Food Culture Must Be Nurtured." *Ottawa Citizen*, June 19, 2012.

———. "The Cutting Edge: The School Where Chefs Are Born." *Ottawa Citizen*, January 12, 2002.

———. "Love Italian Style: A Family of Foodies Builds a Shrine to Their Passion." *Ottawa Citizen*, February 5, 2005.

Chong, Denise. *Lives of the Family: Stories of Fate & Circumstance*. Toronto: Random House Canada, 2013.

Cook, Gay. "Nicastro Family Delivers Again." *Ottawa Citizen*, November 24, 2004.

———. "Signatures Wins Top Dining Award." *Ottawa Citizen*, October 13, 2004.

Costen, Ben. "An Easter Serving of Prime Rib, with Hope on the Side; The Business of Feeding Those Who Required a Hot Meal Was All Too Brisk at the Ottawa Mission Yesterday." *Ottawa Citizen*, March 25, 2008.

Cotton, Larry D. *Whiskey and Wickedness—Rideau River Valley No. 1*. Lanark, ON: Larry D. Cotton Associates Ltd., 2007.

Dar, Patrick. "Not Just Country Folks Upset with the Big City; Some Urban Councillors Say Ottawa Is an Amalgamated City 'That Doesn't Work.'" *Ottawa Citizen*, April 4, 2008.

Deechman, Bruce. "The Shawarma Capital; Ottawa's Streets Are Teeming with Restaurants Selling the Garlicky Middle Eastern Sandwiches." *Ottawa Citizen*, October 31, 2012.

DesBrisay, Anne. "Big-Box Asian Fare Disappoints; Sushi's Fine at Bambu, but Other Fare Flops." *Ottawa Citizen*, March 10, 2011.

———. "Chez Jean Pierre Slips in Consistency." *Ottawa Citizen*, May 20, 1997.

———. "Lunch Pick: Wilf & Ada's on an Entirely New Level." *Ottawa Magazine*, April 28, 2014. http://www.ottawamagazine.com/restaurants/lunch-pick/2014/04/28/wilf-and-adas.

————. "The Pinnacle of French; Signatures Combines Care, Creativity and the Finest of Ingredients." *Ottawa Citizen*, May 13, 2007.

———. "Pizzeria a Grand Addition to ByWard Market." *Ottawa Citizen*, August 13, 2009.

———. "Purring Over Pizza and Pasta." *Ottawa Citizen*, December 17, 2006.

Dimmock, Gary. "Golden Palace Egg Rolls Draw Them from Near and Far; Secret Recipe, Fresh Ingredients and Team of Four Dedicated 'Ladies' Are Keys to Success." *Ottawa Citizen*, December 21, 2009.

———. "On Golden Palace Egg Rolls, 54 Years in Business." *Ottawa Citizen*, April 12, 2014.

Eade, Ron. "A Brasserie Takes Shape, One Bite at a Time." *Ottawa Citizen*, March 2, 2005.

———. "Farewell, Clair de Lune: For Adel Ayad, It's Been a Fun and Fabulous 8,600 Days." *Ottawa Citizen*, December 14, 2005.

———. "Here's the Beef." *Ottawa Citizen*, May 14, 2003.

———. "Le Cordon Bleu Launches Bistro; Students Get Experience; Customers Get a Good Deal." *Ottawa Citizen*, March 6, 2008.

———. "An Orgy for the Taste Buds: Cordon Bleu Cooking School in Ottawa to Open New Restaurant." *Ottawa Citizen*, October 4, 2000.

———. "Ottawa Chefs Capture Awards: They Bring Home 11 Medals from Competition in Scotland." *Ottawa Citizen*, March 28, 2001.

Elliott, Julia. "Popular Restaurateur Makes Bid for Competitor's Location: Deal Expected to Close in Two Weeks." *Ottawa Citizen*, October 1, 1998.

Elmsley, Elizabeth [Kathleen Walker]. "Good Value, No Smoking." *Ottawa Citizen*, June 1, 1990.

———. "Fettucine's: So Deliciously Saucy." *Ottawa Citizen*, October 26, 1990.

———. "Friday's: Any Way You Slice It, Go for Beef." *Ottawa Citizen*, December 31, 1987.

Endemann, Kristin "Cooking for Love; New York Sommelier Returns to Ottawa to Pursue His Passion." *Ottawa Citizen*, April 30, 2004.

Enman, Charles. "Algonquin Culinary Program Founder Began as Chateau Laurier Pot Washer." *Ottawa Citizen*, March 2, 2007.

Flavelle, Dana. "Sign of the Times, Dominion, A&P, the Barn, Ultra Food & Drug, Loeb Renamed." *Toronto Star*, August 8, 2008.

Fotheringham, Allan. "The Cannelloni Accord May Save the Day." *Ottawa Citizen*, November 5, 1981.

Foucault, Marysol, chef/owner, Edgar. Interview and discussion with the authors, March 2014.

Gillies, Majorie. "Agonquin's School of Cooking and Serving." *Ottawa Citizen*, November 27, 1985.

Goff, Kristi. "Cordon Bleu Buys Historic Le Cercle: Restaurant Will Be the First of Its Kind in North America." *Ottawa Citizen*, January 7, 2000.

Grace, Anita. "30 Million Bagels Since '84." *Kitchissippi Times*, April 17, 2014.

Gray, James. "Ritzy Business." *Ottawa Business Life* (May/June 1986).

Guly, Christophere. "The Great Chefs of Prince of Wales Drive: There's a Cordon Bleu School Right Under Our Noses." *Ottawa Citizen*, May 22, 1999.

Haslam, Eugene, owner of Zaphods. Interview and discussion with the authors, February 9, 2014.

Hill, Bert. "Beer: It's a Matter of Taste; Small Beermakers Aren't Too Worried as Big Brewers Try to Tap Their Market." *Ottawa Citizen*, October 30, 1993.

———. "Loeb Stores Renamed in Supermarket Shakeup; Grocer with Ottawa Roots to Carry Metro Moniker." *Ottawa Citizen*, August 8, 2008.

———. "Microbrewery Finds Cure for What Ales It: Montreal Marketer Takes 51% Stake in Hart Breweries." *Ottawa Citizen*, March 5, 1998.

Hill, Sharon. "Fear Smoking Ban, Business Told; Pub Owner Says 20 Months after Ottawa's Bylaw Passed, 38 of 210 Bars Have Shut." *Windsor Star*, April 1, 2003.

Hopper, Tristin. "Party on the Hill: The Favourite Watering Holes of Canada's Parliamentarians." *National Post*, September 15, 2012.

Hum, Peter. "A Little Bit of Heaven on Bank Street." *Ottawa Citizen*, July 21, 1999.

———. "And (Segue) Makes Six." *Ottawa Citizen*, June 5, 2014. http://www2.canada.com/ottawacitizen/news/food/story.html?id=3a6a5eac-9ec6-43d7-866b-262aa97bef50.

———. "Recession Carves Up Another ByWard Landmark." *Ottawa Citizen*, June 2, 1995.

Johnson, Colleen. "Apron Industry." *Dharma Arts*, no. 12 (Fall 2010). http://www.dharmaarts.ca/2010_summer/apron_industry.html?11.

Kainz, Alana. "Hayloft Latest Eatery to Close." *Ottawa Citizen*, January 13, 1993.

Klotz, Hattie. "The Vibe with Peter Boole: Not Long Ago, Ottawa Was a Sorry Place to Venture Out After Dark—Pubs, Taverns or Restaurants that Fed You and Sent You Straight Home Were the Norm. The Scene Has Come a Long Way Since Then, Partly Due to the Vision of Peter Boole, the Man Who Put Some Edge in This City's Nightlife." *Ottawa Citizen*, October 27, 2001.

Korn, Alison. "Thai Food: It's Not for Everyone: Ottawa Restaurateurs Tone Down Fire Factor." *Ottawa Citizen*, February 10, 2001.

Laucius, Joanne. "Three More Smoking Bylaw Convictions: Doc's, Silver Dollar, Star Dance, Each Fined $260." *Ottawa Citizen*, February 13, 2002.

Leblanc, Daniel. "Hull Dull? Partyers Head to Gatineau Ontario Revelers Chase Later Last Call." *Globe and Mail*, October 18, 1999.

Lyprny, Natascia. "College Students Feasting on Food Business; Fewer Are Choosing to Become Auto Mechanics." *Ottawa Citizen*, June 27, 2013.

Mayeda, Andrew. "Lone Star Cooks Up New Growth Plan." *Ottawa Citizen*, June 26, 2004.

May, Kathryn. "Loeb: The Value of a Name; Family Built Grocery Firm Remains a National Force." *Ottawa Citizen*, October 20, 1987.

———. "Lone Star Café; Owners to Mosey on Down the Road with New Chain." *Ottawa Citizen*, May 9, 1989.

———. "Ottawa Valley Brewing Bankrupt." *Ottawa Citizen*, September 8, 1990.

Medd, Paula. "Throwback to a Simpler Era; Farmers' Markets Are a Growth Business in Eastern Ontario." *Ottawa Citizen*, July 23, 1991.

Monga, Vipal. "The Fight to Preserve a Capital Asset." *Globe and Mail*, October 30, 1997.

Mortimer-Proulx, Kyle, former chef at ZenKitchen. Interview and discussion with the authors, April 12, 2014.

Mullington, Dave. "Ottawa Pushed to Fast Track Smoking Bylaw: Medical Officer Wants Target Date Moved Up to 2001." *Ottawa Citizen*, January 26, 2000.

Murray, Maureen. "Cater to Ethnic Shoppers, Grocery Retailers Advised." *Toronto Star*, May 31, 1994.

National Geographic. "Foods to Eat in Ontario." http://travel.nationalgeographic.com/travel/top-10/foods-to-eat-in-ontario/#page=2.

———. "Top 10 Foods to Eat in Ontario." http://travel.nationalgeographic.com/travel/top-10/foods-to-eat-in-ontario/#page=1.

Olijnyk, Zena. "Metro-Richelieu to Buy 41 Loeb Stores Bulk in Ottawa Area." *National Post*, May 4, 1999.

Orton, Marlene. "'Byward Boys' Do It Again: These Bus Boys-Turned-Businessmen Have Had a Hand in Eight Ottawa Eateries, Marlene Orton Reports." Entrepreneurial Spirit: An Occasional Series on Successful Small Business. *Ottawa Citizen*, April 4, 1998.

Ottawa. "101 Must-Try-Before-You-Die Tastes." September 2009.

Ottawa Business Journal. "The Business 'Blinders.'" October 15, 2012.

Ottawa Citizen. "Hull to Get Ottawa-Style Smoking Law." August 22, 1996.

———. "Lovers of Carrot Soup and Liver Pate, Rejoice; William Street Café and Al Pass Along Popular Recipes." March 23, 1988.

Pandi, George. "They Slice, They Score: Canada Brings Back Medals from the World Culinary Olympics. Think of Cooking Competitions as Figure Skating without Scandals." *Ottawa Citizen*, November 30, 2002.

Payne, Elizabeth. "Smoking Bylaw Wins Test; Restaurateur Fined for Not Providing Non-Smoking Section." *Ottawa Citizen*, July 16, 1991.

Pearson, Matthew. "Algonquin Offers New Degree in Hospitality; a Four-Year Program Will Help Students Land Leadership Positions." *Ottawa Citizen*, May 21, 2011.

Pilieci, Vito. "Better Bourguignon than Burgers: But After 20 Years, One of Ottawa's Best-Loved Chefs Is Closing Chez Jean-Pierre." *Ottawa Citizen*, October 11, 2001.

———. "Local Microbrewery Shipped to U.S.; Beau's to Market Two Brews in New York State." *Ottawa Citizen*, January 13, 2014.

Prentice, Michael. "A Fine Taste in Chefs, Certainement." *Ottawa Citizen*, January 8, 2001.

———. "Home on the Range: Cordon Bleu Settles in Ottawa." *Ottawa Citizen*, April 26, 2001.

———. "Let Them Eat Shrimp—About 880 kg." *Ottawa Citizen*, June 12, 1993.

———. "No More Beefs: Friday's Can Stay." *Ottawa Citizen*, August 16, 2003.

Reevely, David. "Ottawa Outdoor Smoking Ban Goes into Effect Monday." *Ottawa Citizen*, April 1, 2003.

Rider, David. "Court Snuffs Out Appeal of Ottawa Smoking Ban: Restaurant and Bar Owners Claim City Went Too Far." *National Post*, May 29, 2002.

———. "Court Upholds Ottawa Smoking Bylaw." *Ottawa Citizen*, May 29. 2002.

Ritchie, Lana G. *Dining Out in Ottawa, Hull, and Environs*. Ottawa: Borealis Press, 1979.

———. *Dining Out in Ottawa, Hull, and Environs*. Ottawa: Borealis Press, 1982.

Robin, Laura. "Brand-New Breweries 100-Mile Beer; HogsBack and Kichesippi Promise Pints of Local Flavour." *Ottawa Citizen*, June, 10 2010.

Rupert, Jake. "82 Eateries Open Despite Ban on Smoking: Study: Councilor Argues Bar, Restaurant Business Is Booming; Coalition Says Bylaw Is Choking Members." *Ottawa Citizen*, May 6, 2002.

———. "'I Needed This to Support My Family': City Bylaw Forces Father of Seven Out of Hotdog Business." *Ottawa Citizen*, April 19, 1998.

———. "Smoking Violations Cost Bar $37,895: City Open to Negotiating Lesser Fine if Tavern Starts to Obey Bylaw." *Ottawa Citizen*, September 10, 2002.

Rural Summit. "Rural Summit: 2005 Initiatives." City of Ottawa. http://ottawa.ca/en/rural-summits-0.

Scanlan, David. "Market Tax Revolt; ByWard Merchants Fear Hikes Will Drive Them Out." *Ottawa Citizen*, July 16, 1992.

Schultz, Judy. "Lone Star Shines, No Flavoured Coffee at Starbuck's." *Edmonton Journal*, August 27, 1997.

Silcoff, Sean. "Repeat Success: After Gourmet Burger Score, Can Restaurateur Do the Same with Pizza?" *Globe and Mail*, July 6, 2012. http://www.theglobeandmail.com/report-on-business/small-business/sb-growth/success-stories/after-gourmet-burger-score-can-restaurateur-do-the-same-with-pizza/article4394753.

Smith, Marie-Danielle. "Golden Beer Tunnel Memories; Arnprior Man, 91, Worked in Area Uncovered by Albert St. Construction." *Ottawa Citizen*, July 5, 2014.

Sneath, Allen Winn. *Brewed in Canada*. Toronto: Dundurn, 2001.

Spalding, Derek. "How an Empire Was Built; Ottawa Business Owners Dominate the Specialty Dining Market." *Ottawa Citizen*, April 13, 2013.

Spang, Rebecca L. *The Invention of the Restaurant*. Cambridge, MA: Harvard University Press, 2000.

Spears, Tom, and Melanie Brooks. "Terrible for Ottawa, Good for Us: Hull Bar Owners 'Very Happy' About Anti-Smoking Bylaw." *Ottawa Citizen*, April 8, 2001.

Standen, Karyn. "Last-Minute Deal Saves Dining Landmark." *Ottawa Citizen*, July 25, 1998, D1.

Stanyar, Barbara. "IGA Leads Loblaws in Price War." *Ottawa Citizen*, March 20, 1986.

Statistics Canada. "2011 Farm and Farm Operator Data." 2011 Census of Agriculture, Farm and Farm Operator Data. http://www29.statcan.gc.ca/ceag-web/eng/community-agriculture-profile-profil-agricole.action?geoId=350406008&selectedVarIds=350%2C351%2C.

Stein, Kyrn, chef, Social Restaurant and Lounge. Interview and discussion with the authors, March 2014.

Stratton, Jane. "Where's the Beef? Not in These Burgers." *Ottawa Citizen*, September 6, 2000.

Sutherland, Anne. "Tobacco Banned? It's Not So Bad, Ottawa's Pub Milieu Discovered." *Gazette*, May 14, 2005.

Taylor, John H. *Ottawa: An Illustrated History*. Toronto: James Lorimer & Company and Canadian Museum of Civilization, 1986.

Ten Holder, Wim ten Hagen. *Café Wim: A Touch of Dutch on Sussex Drive*. Ottawa: Arbour House, 2009.

Toronto Star. "Le Cordon Bleu Cooking School to Open Ottawa Branch." From the Canadian Press, June 29, 1988.

TripAdvisor. "Ottawa Restaurants." http://www.tripadvisor.ca/Restaurants-g155004-Ottawa_Ontario.html.

Van Dusen, Tom. "A Beau Market for Organic Beer." *Ottawa Su*, July 9, 2009.

Walker, Kathleen. "Banned! Ritz Owner Won't Allow Smoking at Three Restaurants." *Ottawa Citizen*, May 30, 1990.

———. "The Birth of the Chip Wagons: Even in Early Bytown, Street Vendors Were Dogged by Red Tape." Series: A Taste of History. *Ottawa Citizen*, July 12, 1995.

———. "Cindy Yabar's Secret Is Dedication to a Dream." *Ottawa Citizen*, February 7, 1996.

———. "Cordon Bleu Chefs' Course Comes to Canada." *Ottawa Citizen*, August 3, 1988.

———. "Guest Chefs: Today, the Citizen Continues an Occasional Series Profiling Some of the Talented Chefs in the Ottawa Area. Each Will Share a Recipe Illustrated with a Series of How-To Photos. Today, in the Second of the Series, Food Editor Kathleen Walker Talks to Art Akarapanich of Sweet Basil." *Ottawa Citizen*, March 20, 1996.

———. "Hayloft Changes Hands While Victor's Restaurant to Close Doors." *Ottawa Citizen*, July 27, 1988.

———. "1975–1985: Ottawa Discovers Dining Out Series: A Taste of History." *Ottawa Citizen*, September 13, 1995.

———. *Ottawa's Repast: 150 Years of Food and Drink*. Ottawa: Ottawa Citizen, 1995.

———. "Ritz 3 Owner Expands Menu to Add New Take-Out Store." *Ottawa Citizen*, February 27, 1991.

Ward, Bruce. "How Ottawans Saved 4000 People in Distress: A New Book Recounts How Then-Mayor Marion Dewar Rallied a Community to Respond to the 1979 Refugee Crisis." *Ottawa Citizen*, May 3, 2008.

———. "The Half-Price Egg Rolls Sold Like Hotcakes; Golden Palace's Fans Snapped Up 5,000 Deep-Fried Treats to Mark Its Anniversary." *Ottawa Citizen*, April 14, 2011.

Ward, Peter. "The Ritz Makes Own Wine with Very Tasty Results." *Ottawa Citizen*, January 29, 1992.

Wheeler, Carolynne. "Courts Upholds No-Smoking Bylaw: PUBCO Vows to Appeal; Mayor Celebrates Victory." *Ottawa Citizen*, September 1, 2001.

Winston, Iris. "Nicastro's Make It Personal: Owner of Food Emporium Boosts Business by Taking Good Care of His Customers." Series: Entrepreneurial Spirit: A Series on Successful Small Business. *Ottawa Citizen*, January 22, 2000.

INDEX

P

R

S

T

U

W

Y

Z

ABOUT THE AUTHORS

Both born and raised in Ottawa, Ontario, Don Chow and Jennifer Lim grew up in families where food was the centre of family and holiday celebrations.

Don's inspiration for cooking came from his parents, who instilled in their children a love for earth-to-table eating. They had a garden in the backyard growing up, and he and his sisters learned what vegetables taste like when not shipped for hours in refrigerated trucks. Don's family also shopped in ethnic and farmers' markets, opening his eyes to different foods from a young age.

For Jennifer, her love for food and cooking developed when she used to complete her homework at the kitchen table while her mother prepared the family meals. Her parents also had their own vegetable garden in the backyard and involved the children in taking care of it. Some of her favourite childhood memories are grocery shopping with her parents, baking cakes and Hong Kong–style buns with her mother and watching fish and shrimp swim in tanks at the seafood stores in Vancouver, British Columbia.

In December 2006, Don founded foodiePrints, with Jennifer officially joining him as editor and blogger one year later. Initially, it was meant to be a collection of recipes, but soon it grew into a collection of stories and reviews of restaurants. They learned that their hometown prepared and served great food. From meeting restaurateurs, chefs, cooks, farmers and other local producers, they have been documenting it all and sharing it with their readers around the world.

When they are not blogging, cooking or shopping for groceries, Don can be found practicing his photography skills, while Jennifer trains for long-distance running in the forest, hoping to find wild berries along the way.